Robyn Lawley
eats

Robyn Lawley
eats

EBURY
PRESS

This book is dedicated to all my friends,
who helped me in payment of food,

To my agent, Chelsea,
for believing in me,

To my sisters, Shona and Jennifer,
who inspire me,

To my parents, for loving me,

To my grandma, Mutti,
for forever motivating me,

And to my one true love, Everest:
without you, everything just falls apart.

Contents

'There is no love sincerer than the love of food'

– George Bernard Shaw

MY LOVE FOR COOKING began before I can even remember. One of my earliest memories is convincing my mum to place a stool near the kitchen bench so I could help her mix a chocolate cake. And at another time, on a different stool, making rissoles and laughing at the mess on my hands. I knew, even from that young age, that food and cooking would be a huge part of my life.

When I was a little older, my family would often turn to me to cook a family meal or dessert. My mother was an inspiring mentor for me when it came to cooking. She would let me run amok in the kitchen and allowed me to cook anything I wanted, while giving advice along the way. I baked lemon meringue pies for my grandma, mulberry tarts for my sisters, fish and chips for dinner and chocolate cakes for everyone's birthdays. Birthday cakes were always my favourite to make. To further my cake decorating dreams, I took a cake decorating class when I was 12 years old. I would make big bouquets of flowers and paint them all different colours. It was edible art – I was hooked.

I was often the first home, and during the only quiet hour in my household, I would pretend to be a chef on a cooking show while I prepared meals. I'm glad no one stumbled in on me while I was indicating to my invisible audience how one kneads dough.

I collected countless recipes with my mum, including the recipes from all her old cookbooks, some so old and worn that the pages were stuck together forever, lost in mulberry jam.

My family became used to my obsession. The running joke was that at breakfast, I'd ask, 'What's for dinner?'

I begged to be taken to restaurants – my Aunty Wendy in Melbourne took me to plenty whenever I visited. As I devoured every meal I imagined and memorised what the chef had done and how they cooked it so that I could experiment when I got back home.

IN MY TEENAGE YEARS, before I even thought of modelling as a career option, I had aspirations to become a chef. I studied food technology, took TAFE hospitality classes and worked at various restaurants. I dreamt of being accepted into Le Cordon Bleu, an acclaimed cooking school in France, and opening my own restaurant.

In my teens I also became a strict vegan, for ethical/environmental reasons and as a means of controlling my diet, as I wanted to lose weight to model. It was a new world. I had to learn how to cook all my recipes to vegan standards. There were zero vegan restaurants where I lived, and the term was completely foreign to most people. I kept it mostly secret. Looking back, I don't know how someone like me, whose main love is food, gave up cheese for three years. I distinctively remember an upper-class restaurant in Terrigal, New South Wales, that brought their head chef out to ask me what a vegan ate. They served me the biggest pile of sliced tomatoes I had ever seen, and nothing else. But my mother was up for the challenge and she became quite the vegan cook. We learnt how to make cakes without eggs, using pureed vegetables instead, similar to my vegan cupcakes in this cookbook, which are utterly delicious and completely animal-free.

EVEN THOUGH I WAS VEGAN, I continued with my cooking classes. My love of food is what led me to France on a year-long exchange trip when I was 17. Not only did I want to learn another language, but I also wanted to live (and eat!) like a French person.

I noticed that people in France often ate seasonally with homegrown vegetables. They would shop a few times a week at local markets. My French host mother, Aline, purchased fresh bread daily. I should reiterate – my French host mother, Aline, purchased delicious, warm, fresh bread daily. I was in a food lover's paradise.

Having access to such fresh produce was a dream for me. I arrived in France a straight-sized model and by the time I returned home I was a plus-sized model. There was a huge amount of food I had to suddenly be comfortable with after spending years denying myself (by now I was no longer vegan).

I witnessed my French host brother, Florent, guzzle chocolate milk and brioche every morning and my French host dad, JoJo, had the biggest Nutella jar I had ever seen. The jar would taunt me daily and soon I realised that Nutella would forever remain an addiction.

It was impossible to ignore the produce there. I would often buy goat's cheese that was made by local farmers who raised their goats on a certain mountain so they could eat a certain grass in order to produce their particular type of cheese.

Quality in the produce you cook makes all the difference. Even though I eat meat now I'm still very much against factory farming and animal cruelty. I'm also not a fan of diet, fat-free or packaged foods with too many additives. To me this is 'fake' food.

A FEW YEARS AFTER MY FRENCH EXCHANGE and travelling around the world, I ended up living in New York, which I've made my home base for the last five years.

During my first two years in New York I think I ate out every day. Sometimes breakfast, brunch, lunch and dinner. It was so extravagant. New Yorkers mainly do it because grocery shopping without a car is inconvenient, not to mention expensive, and most people only have incredibly small, closet-like kitchens that limit storage – shoes kept in the oven, for example. New York also has such a huge array of endless restaurant options beckoning to your desire.

I lived in Williamsburg, Brooklyn, where restaurants were not only excellent and unique but also incredibly cheap.

I feature an array of 'American New' food in this cookbook.

The inspiration to start a food blog began during my second year in New York. I decided to start capturing the food I ate. I was travelling everywhere around the world and I thought it would be great to keep a food journal, an exciting way to remember all the delicious dishes I was enjoying. I started the blog *Robyn Lawley Eats* shortly thereafter and, looking back on it now, it was one of the best decisions I have made. It was great to see all my photos accruing and people's reactions to the food I posted. I would visit food markets and restaurants I liked, photograph their food and leave behind calling cards saying, 'You've been blogged.'

I'd been living in Williamsburg for three years when I felt a need for change – and more space. I moved to the financial district in Manhattan, right near Wall Street, but when I arrived I was suddenly confronted with a neighbourhood where the food had no soul, much to my dismay. Hurricane Sandy had destroyed most of the seaport, parks and restaurants close to me, and eating out all the time became difficult.

Since one of the reasons I'd moved was for a better kitchen, I took it upon myself to cook more and to go grocery shopping a few times a week, just like the French. I felt like I was the only person in New York who needed a large trolley for groceries at Wholefoods, or who would carry ten bags by hand on the train back from the Union Square markets.

THIS COOKBOOK IS A JOURNEY similar to that of my blog. It's food that has mattered to me. Everything in this cookbook is also photographed, then eaten, by me and my partner (to the dismay of our belts). There's no trick photography or fake sprays, just real food I cooked at home, in my tiny kitchen, with a bad oven.

To eat the vast amount of food I had to cook, I would constantly invite my friends over. And here lies the best thing about food: it brings people together. There's a huge amount of love that goes into a home-cooked meal. My favourite restaurant in New York is now my kitchen, and I relish the times I can share these wonderful meals with my friends. There's a reason why I'll give the best food to my friends and save the scraps for myself. I have no love higher than the gift of sharing food.

I hope you find these recipes give you many moments of joy that you can share with your friends and family, like they have for me. Don't forget to experiment and have fun. I always try to give recipes my own touch. To help, I have included some pages with room where you can write your individual notes about the recipes – that way, you can truly make this cookbook your own.

Yours very truly,
Robyn

www.robynlawleyeats.tumblr.com

A BRIEF BUT IMPORTANT NOTE ABOUT
FARMING PRACTICES

Farming has changed dramatically over the past 40 years. Today we have very few farms where animals can roam freely. Meat production is mainly done behind closed doors and is known as factory farming, controlled by big corporations. Over 500 million animals are raised for food in factory farms every year, in Australia alone.

These animals aren't legally seen as animals but as 'property' under Australian law. I encourage my readers when buying groceries, especially meat, poultry, dairy and eggs, to buy as ethically as possible. Too often we don't know where our produce is from. Local markets and farms offer personal insight to their treatment of animals and offer better alternatives. Industrialised farming practices are terrible to animals and also create poorer quality meat as they do not eat grass or, in most cases, even see sunlight. I know not everyone has access to more sustainable produce, but just be actively aware and do what you can. You will feel better about it and it will taste better.

Australian Heartache

There is just something about all these recipes that instantly makes me happy. I suppose it's nostalgia. They are recipes I have grown up with or expected at family gatherings. Whenever I am back in Australia I beg my mum to make all my favourites. Even though I love to cook, I still relish my mother's meals. Living abroad, I constantly make these meals for my friends. Sometimes I have brought them to my agency. It's fun to introduce Americans to foods they have no idea about, like lamingtons or pavlova.

I hope you enjoy making these classics. Make sure to try the mulberry tart recipe. It was the first tart I ever made, and the one thing my family still begs me to make.

Bircher muesli

I often have to make my own muesli in America as it can be difficult to find cereal without added sugar or corn syrup. My favourite type is Bircher muesli and this recipe below is an absolute winner.

PREPARATION TIME: 10 MINUTES + OVERNIGHT SOAKING
SERVES: 2

1 apple (gala, pink lady or granny smith)
1 cup rolled oats
1/2 cup apple juice
3 dried dates, chopped
1/2 cup plain yoghurt, plus extra to serve
large pinch ground cinnamon
1/4 cup flaked almonds
1/4 cup roughly chopped walnuts
blueberries or raspberries, to serve

1. Coarsely grate the apple, leaving the core. Mix the grated apple, rolled oats, apple juice, dates, yoghurt and cinnamon in a bowl until combined. Cover and refrigerate overnight.
2. Combine the flaked almonds and walnuts in a small bowl.
3. Stir half the nut mixture through the muesli. Top with the remaining nut mixture and serve with blueberries or raspberries and a little extra yoghurt.

NOTE: Bircher muesli is traditionally soaked overnight, but if you want to make this on the day you want to eat it, refrigerate for at least an hour.

Pikelets

I prefer pikelets to pancakes – to me they just have a better consistency. It only took one morning for me to steer my partner away from pancakes and towards the Australian pikelet.

PREPARATION TIME: 10 MINUTES
COOKING TIME: 10–15 MINUTES
MAKES: ABOUT 20, DEPENDING ON THE SIZE

2 cups self-raising flour
3–5 tbsp caster sugar, depending on how sweet you want them
1 1/2 cups milk
2 eggs
1 vanilla bean, split, seeds removed
50g butter

1. Sift the flour and sugar together in a bowl.
2. Whisk the milk, eggs and vanilla seeds together, then add to the dry ingredients, whisking until it reaches a smooth consistency.
3. Melt a little bit of butter in a large non-stick frying pan over medium heat. Drop tablespoons of batter into the pan (I use a ladle), but don't overcrowd the pan. When the surface starts to bubble, flip them over. Remove once they have turned golden on both sides.
4. Don't fret if the first batch doesn't turn out perfectly (just do a couple to start with). It usually takes one go to get the temperature right in the frying pan. Repeat with remaining batter in batches.
5. Serve with your choice of topping. My favourite is Nutella and banana, but another good serving option is fresh lemon juice and a sprinkle of sugar.

TRICK: Warm the vanilla bean gently in your hands before extracting the seeds with the back of a knife.

Watermelon and rocket salad

This salad is a summer favourite – all these flavours mixed together makes it seriously delicious!

PREPARATION TIME: 15 MINUTES
SERVES: 2

1 medium red onion, halved and finely sliced
80g feta or goat's cheese, crumbled
$\frac{1}{4}$ watermelon, cut into chunks
100g baby rocket leaves (2–3 handfuls)
1 tbsp pine nuts

Dressing:

1 tbsp olive oil
1 tbsp white vinegar
3 tsp lemon juice
3 tsp wholegrain mustard
1 tsp mayonnaise, plus an extra tsp to thicken, if desired

1. Combine all the salad ingredients in a bowl or on a platter.
2. To make the dressing, combine all the ingredients in a small bowl and whisk until smooth (or throw into a sealed jar and shake).
3. Just before serving, drizzle salad with dressing and toss to combine.

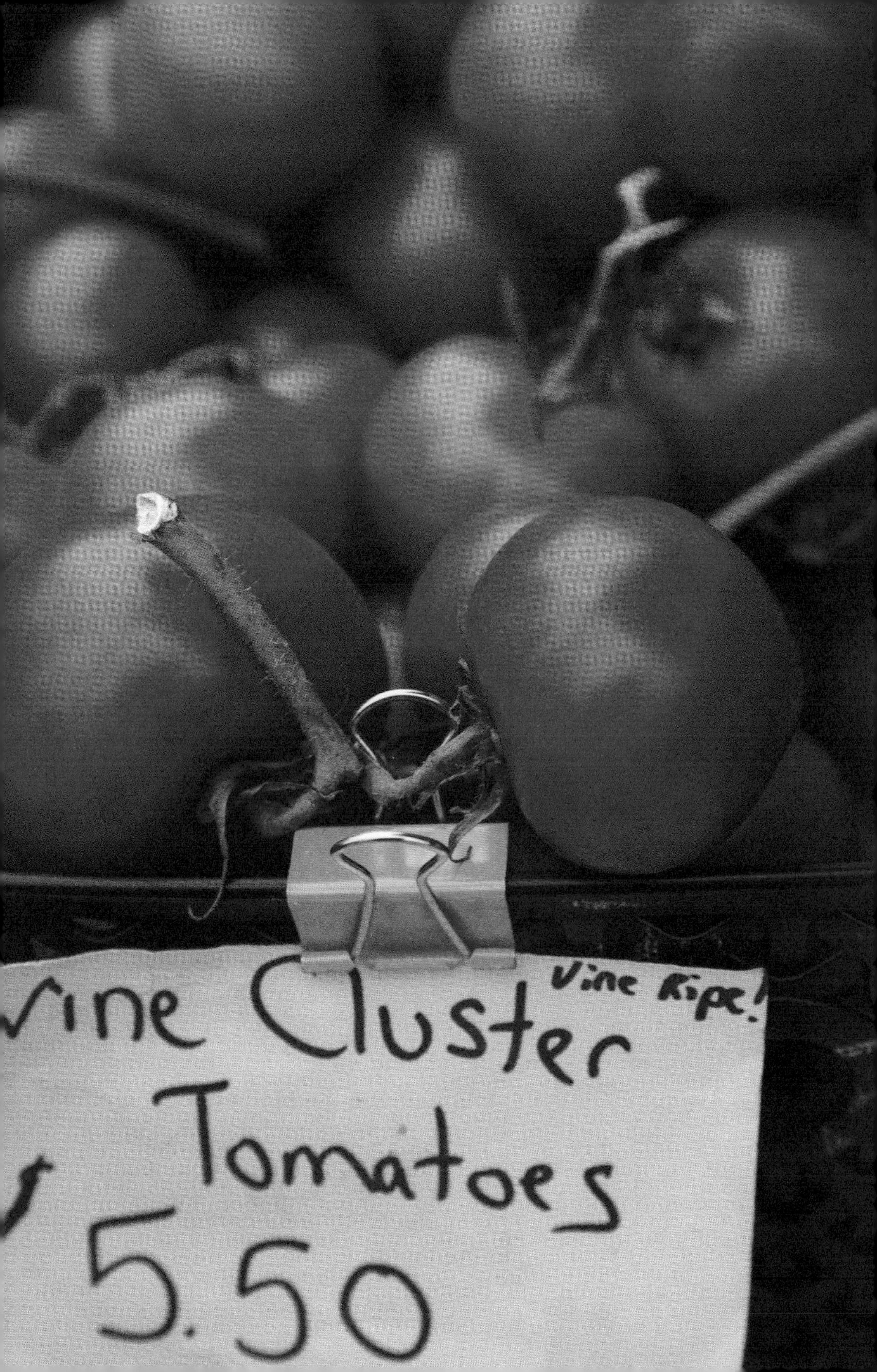
Vine Ripe!
vine Cluster
Tomatoes
5.50

Buffalo salad

Mozzarella and tomato are just such a great combination, and the added saltiness of the anchovies takes this recipe to a new level.

4 large buffalo mozzarella balls
16 basil leaves
16 small anchovy fillets (leave out if you dislike anchovies, or for a vegetarian dish)
24 cherry tomatoes, halved
$1/2$ cup lemon juice
2 tbsp olive oil
sea salt and freshly cracked pepper to taste
balsamic vinegar and extra olive oil, to serve

1. Slice each ball of mozzarella into 4 even slices. Place a slice of mozzarella onto each of four plates. Top with a basil leaf, an anchovy fillet and 3-4 halves of cherry tomato. Repeat layering so you have stacks with four layers of each ingredient on each plate.
2. Drizzle the olive oil and lemon juice over all the stacks.
3. Sprinkle sea salt flakes and cracked pepper on top, and serve with balsamic vinegar and extra olive oil on the side.

Potato salad

My mum has made this dish for every barbecue and every house party I've ever had. I love it so much. It's a staple addition to any gathering, delicious, and can easily be made vegetarian by skipping the ham.

PREPARATION TIME: 25 MINUTES
COOKING TIME: 15 MINUTES
SERVES: 8–10

6-8 potatoes (about 1kg)
5 eggs
1 cup diced ham (off the bone)
1 cup mayonnaise
$^1/_4$ tsp salt
1 tbsp chives (fresh or dried)
1 tsp dill (fresh or dried)
$^1/_4$ tsp garlic powder

1. Peel the potatoes and cut into small cubes, then microwave for 8-10 minutes (alternatively, boil until just soft). Once cooked, rinse with cold water and set aside.
2. While you boil the potatoes, boil the eggs for 15 minutes, then rinse with cold water afterwards. This prevents the yolk from browning.
3. Once the potatoes and eggs have cooled, place into a large bowl and add the ham. Add the mayonnaise, salt, chives and dill. Sprinkle the garlic powder over and gently fold through. Serve cold.

Bean salad

PREPARATION TIME: 20 MINUTES + CHILLING
SERVES: 6–8

425g can black beans, rinsed and drained
425g can kidney beans, rinsed and drained
425g can cannellini beans, rinsed and drained
280g can corn kernels, drained
1 green capsicum, chopped
1 yellow capsicum, chopped
1 red capsicum, chopped
1 red onion, chopped
1/2 cup extra virgin olive oil
1/2 cup red wine vinegar
2 tbsp fresh lime juice
1 tbsp lemon juice
1 garlic clove, crushed
1/2 cup chopped fresh coriander
3 spring onions, chopped
1 tsp sugar
2 tsp ground black pepper
1 fresh red chilli, chopped
1 dash Tabasco

1. In a large bowl, combine the beans, corn, capsicum and red onion.
2. In a small bowl, whisk together the olive oil, red wine vinegar, lime juice, lemon juice, garlic, coriander, spring onions, sugar and black pepper. Add chilli and season with Tabasco and salt to taste.
3. Pour the dressing over the beans and vegetables. Fold through until combined. Chill thoroughly, and serve cold.

Curried couscous

PREPARATION TIME: 20 MINUTES
COOKING TIME: 5 MINUTES + 5 MINUTES STANDING
SERVES: 4–6 AS A SIDE DISH

2 tbsp olive oil
1 small red onion, diced
2 garlic cloves, crushed
10 cherry tomatoes, halved
10 pitted kalamata olives, halved
1$\frac{1}{2}$ cups couscous
3 cups water (or chicken stock for extra flavour)
2 tsp curry powder
40g sultanas
$\frac{1}{2}$ teaspoon salt and cracked black pepper
$\frac{1}{2}$ cup fresh coriander leaves

1. Heat 1 tablespoon of oil in a pan and lightly fry the onion, garlic, tomatoes and olives until softened; set aside. Put the couscous into a heatproof bowl.

2. Combine the water or chicken stock, curry powder, sultanas, remaining olive oil and salt and pepper in a saucepan and bring to the boil. Remove from the heat and pour over the couscous. Cover and stand for 5 minutes or until all the liquid has been absorbed.

3. Once the couscous has fully absorbed the liquid, fluff with a fork, then toss in the onion mixture. Add the fresh coriander and mix all the ingredients with a fork.

    NOTE: This dish can be served hot or cold. Pine nuts or almonds are optional, if you want to add some extra crunch. I recommend serving with grilled or pan-fried salmon, lemon wedges, and a dollop of tzatziki on top.

Pumpkin soup

I implore you to make this pumpkin soup! It's fresh and easy and perfect to make for a loved one who has a cold. My mum made this for my sisters and me when we were kids, and we still remember how heartwarming it was.

PREPARATION TIME: 15 MINUTES
COOKING TIME: 20 MINUTES
SERVES: 2

$1/2$ butternut or Aussie sunset pumpkin (700g), peeled, seeds removed
2 medium carrots
2 tbsp stock powder (vegetable or chicken)
1 tbsp olive oil
1 large brown onion, chopped
1 garlic clove, crushed
plain yoghurt and chopped parsley, optional, to serve
sea salt and fresh cracked pepper, to taste

1. Chop the pumpkin and carrots and fold through the stock powder in a bowl.
2. Heat the oil in a large saucepan and fry the onions and garlic until lightly browned. Add the remaining vegetables and brown slightly, then add 6 cups of water.
3. Bring to boil, then simmer for 15 minutes. Cool slightly, then using a stick blender, blend all ingredients until the consistency is smooth.
4. If you like, serve with a dollop of yoghurt and a sprinkle of parsley.

Pan-fried salmon

Salmon is one of those dishes that is so easy but often gets overcooked.
You can literally have salmon ready to go within 10 minutes.

PREPARATION TIME: 10 MINUTES
COOKING TIME: 5 MINUTES
SERVES: HOWEVER MANY YOU LIKE!

1 piece of salmon fillet per person, skin on
For each piece of salmon:
2 tsp wholegrain mustard
1 tsp chopped chives
$1/4$ tsp finely grated lemon zest
$1/2$ tsp extra virgin olive oil
sea salt and lemon slices, to serve

1. Combine the mustard, chives and lemon zest and rub gently with your fingers
   all over the salmon. Season with salt and freshly ground black pepper.
2. Heat the oil in a large frying pan until hot, then fry the salmon skin side down
   for 3 minutes – you want it slightly crispy on that side only.
3. Turn and fry for another 2–3 minutes (be careful not to overcook).
4. Serve immediately, seasoned with sea salt, with a slice of lemon.

Tuna pasta bake

This is what I consider comfort food. My mum has been making different types of pasta bakes our whole lives. It's simple and easy to make for a family and is great as leftovers. In fact, I prefer eating this pasta bake the next day.

PREPARATION TIME: 20 MINUTES
COOKING TIME: 30 MINUTES
SERVES: 5

600g penne or macaroni
200g bacon (or prosciutto), finely chopped
80g butter
$\frac{1}{2}$ cup plain flour
600ml milk
400g strong vintage cheddar, grated
2 x 160g cans tuna, drained and flaked
330g can sweetcorn, drained
6 broccoli florets, halved (optional)
large handful chopped flat-leaf parsley
1 tsp garlic powder
1 cup grated parmesan

1. Preheat the oven to 180°C and grease a 10-cup capacity baking dish.
2. Bring a large saucepan of salted water to the boil and add the pasta. Cook unti just before al dente, and drain. Meanwhile, cook the bacon in a frying pan until crisp.
3. Melt the butter in a saucepan. Add the flour and cook, stirring, for 1 minute. Gradually add the milk and keep stirring until the sauce boils and thickens. Remove from heat and stir in about half the cheddar.
4. Mix the sauce with the drained pasta and add the bacon, corn, broccoli and parsley. Season with garlic powder, salt and freshly ground black pepper to taste.
5. Transfer to the baking dish and sprinkle the parmesan and remaining cheddar on top. Add a little more garlic powder. Bake for 15–20 minutes, until the cheese is golden.

NOTE: If you have mozzarella or gruyère handy, you can sprinkle on top with the other cheeses. If you have time, the best way to cook the bacon is in the oven. Preheat oven to 200°C. Wash the bacon under cold water (this helps it retain its shape and size). Place onto a wire rack over a baking tray and cook for 20 minutes or until crisp.

Spicy sunset fettuccine with prawns and lemon

PREPARATION TIME: 15 MINUTES
COOKING TIME: 10 MINUTES
SERVES: 4

500g dried or fresh fettuccine
2 tbsp olive oil
3 garlic cloves, peeled and chopped
16 tiger prawns, peeled and deveined
150g cherry tomatoes, halved
2–3 red chillies, deseeded and chopped (optional)
2 tsp finely grated lemon zest
$\frac{1}{2}$ cup rocket leaves
$\frac{1}{4}$ cup coriander leaves
sea salt and fresh cracked pepper to taste
to garnish:
shaved parmesan
lemon wedges

1. Bring a large saucepan of water to the boil and add a good pinch of salt. Add the fettuccine and cook until al dente (prepare the pasta before you cook the prawns as it does not take long). Drain.
2. When the pasta is almost al dente, heat $\frac{1}{2}$ tablespoon of olive oil in a large deep frying pan and cook the garlic and prawns until the prawns change colour. Add the tomatoes, chilli and lemon zest, stir-fry for another minute.
3. Add the rocket and coriander, then add the fettuccine to the prawns and mix well. Season with salt and pepper.
4. Garnish with the parmesan and lemon wedges. Drizzle remaining olive oil over pasta.

NOTE: If using fresh fettuccine, be aware that it will take less time to cook than dried fettuccine, so plan accordingly.

If your pasta is ready and waiting, a simple drizzle of olive oil and a stir-through prevents the pasta from sticking and drying out.

Devils on horseback

One of my favourite restaurants in New York is called Five Leaves, in Green Point, Brooklyn. The restaurant was the brainchild of the late Heath Ledger with business partners Scott Campbell and Jud Mongell.

They have an amazing Australian/American influenced menu, and the yummiest appetiser on their menu is called Devils on Horseback. A simple idea and easy construction, but a decadent masterpiece.

PREPARATION TIME: 20 MINUTES
COOKING TIME: 20–25 MINUTES
SERVES: 6

12 thick-cut bacon rashers, halved crosswise
24 large dates, pitted
Dijon mustard, to serve

1. Preheat the oven to 200°C. Line a baking tray with baking paper. Place 24 toothpicks in a bowl filled with water and soak for 15 minutes.
2. Wrap a piece of bacon around each date and secure with a toothpick. Place dates onto the lined tray. Bake for about 20–25 minutes, until bacon is cooked through.
3. Serve with the Dijon mustard.

NOTE: You could stuff the dates with a little bit of goat's cheese if you like.

Beer-battered fish & chips

PREPARATION TIME: 25 MINUTES
COOKING TIME: 40 MINUTES
SERVES: 5–6

Chips:

6 desiree potatoes, cut into wedges (peeling is optional)
2 tbsp olive oil
leaves from 2 rosemary sprigs
sea salt and freshly ground black pepper, to taste

Beer-battered fish:

2$\frac{1}{2}$ cups self-raising flour
1 egg, lightly whisked
375ml (1$\frac{1}{2}$ cups) chilled light beer
vegetable oil, to deep-fry
$\frac{1}{3}$ cup plain flour, extra
1 tsp paprika
1 tsp garlic powder
8 (about 120g each) white fish fillets, such as flathead or whiting
sea salt flakes, to serve
lemon wedges, to serve

1. For the chips, preheat the oven to 210°C, and line 2 large baking trays with baking paper. Put the potato into a plastic bag. Add the olive oil and rosemary, and season with the sea salt and freshly ground black pepper. Seal the opening and shake the bag until the chips are evenly coated.

2. Lay out on the trays and bake for about 40 minutes, turning once during cooking so they cook evenly. They should look nice and golden and be a little crispy.

3. Meanwhile, to make the beer-battered fish, place the self-raising flour into a bowl and whisk in the egg. Slowly add the beer, whisking gently to combine. Whisk in a pinch of salt and place into the fridge to rest for 20 minutes.

4. Half fill a large saucepan (or deep-fryer) with oil and heat over high heat.

5. Combine the plain flour, paprika and garlic powder on a plate and season with salt and freshly ground black pepper. Working a few at a time to avoid overcrowding the pan, dip the fish fillets into the flour mixture, making sure it's completely coated. Dip into the batter. Immediately after fish is coated with batter, lower into the hot oil.

6. Cook for 3–4 minutes, or until the fish has turned a nice golden colour and floats to the surface. Lift out with a slotted spoon and drain on paper towels.

7. Serve the beer-battered fish and chips seasoned with sea salt, and with lemon wedges to squeeze over the fish.

Braised lamb chops

PREPARATION TIME: 15 MINUTES
COOKING TIME: APPROX. 1 HOUR 15 MINUTES
SERVES: 4

This was one of my favorite meals growing up. Much to my dismay, my mum would only cook this on special occasions, such as when people came and stayed with us from out of town. The meat becomes so tender that the lamb literally melts in your mouth.

1. Preheat the oven to 180°C. Lightly dust the lamb chops with flour and shake off the excess. Melt half the butter in a frying pan and brown both sides of the lamb chops.
2. Remove excess fat by patting the chops dry with paper towels, then place into a large casserole dish. Wipe out the frying pan with paper towel.
3. Melt the remaining butter in the frying pan and cook the onion until it browns slightly. Add the wine and stock and stir constantly until the sauce thickens slightly. Pour over the chops. Cover and cook for about 40 minutes, until very tender.
4. Meanwhile, peel the potatoes and boil until almost soft, then drain and cut into thick slices. Sauté the mushrooms in butter and season with salt. Scatter the potatoes, mushrooms and frozen peas over the lamb chops and bake for a further 30 minutes.

4 lamb forequarter chops
small amount of plain flour to
    coat the chops
2 tbsp salted butter
1 large onion, finely sliced
$^1/_4$ cup white wine
$^3/_4$ cup stock (vegetable or beef)
4 medium potatoes
1 cup sliced mushrooms
2 tsp butter, extra
1 cup frozen peas

1 whole chicken
2 brown onions, quartered
2 garlic cloves, crushed
2 lemons, quartered
small bunch of thyme
150g butter, melted
$1/2$ tsp finely grated lemon zest
$1/2$ tsp salt
$1/2$ tsp cracked pepper

Chicken roast

I always love a dinner party and I usually pop a roast on. It's a crowd pleaser and once in the oven you can focus on getting everything else ready.

PREPARATION TIME: 15 MINUTES
COOKING TIME: $1^1/2$ HOURS
SERVES: 6

1. Preheat the oven to 180°C.
2. Pat the chicken dry with paper towels. Place the onion, garlic, lemon and thyme inside the chicken.
3. Mix the melted butter with lemon zest, salt and pepper. Spread over the outside of the chicken to evenly coat it, but keep a little bit aside so you can baste it throughout the cooking process.
4. Place the chicken in a roasting pan (if you are roasting vegetables, you can place them around or under the chicken). Roast for $1-1^1/2$ hours, depending on the size of the chicken.
5. To check that it's cooked through, pierce the chicken through the drumstick. If the juices run clear, it is cooked. When done, remove from the oven, cover with foil and rest for 15 minutes. This allows the moisture to be reabsorbed back into the chicken.

NOTE: If you microwave a lemon for 30 seconds, the flavour will be a lot stronger. You can use olive oil instead of melted butter if you like.

Honey soy chicken wings

These chicken wings are a party favourite – juicy and easy to make.

PREPARATION TIME: 10 MINUTES + 1 HOUR MARINATING
COOKING TIME: 35–40 MINUTES
MAKES: 12 CHICKEN WINGS

12 chicken wings
3–4 tbsp soy sauce
1 tbsp teriyaki sauce
1 tbsp tomato sauce
1 tbsp honey
2 tsp crushed garlic

1. Pat the wings dry with paper towels and place them into a shallow casserole dish.
2. Combine the remaining ingredients in a jar and pour over the wings, making sure the wings are evenly coated. Cover and place into the fridge for at least 1 hour to marinate. Remove from the fridge 15 minutes before cooking, so the chicken isn't quite so chilled when it goes into the oven.
3. Preheat the oven to 180°C. Cook the chicken in the casserole dish for 35–40 minutes, depending on chicken wing size. The casserole dish helps the marinade really soak in while cooking, compared to a roasting tray.

NOTE: The longer you can marinate the chicken, the better the flavour will be. Five hours would be ideal.

Pot roast chicken marylands with spring vegetables

I love how juicy the chicken is with this recipe – not quite a soup, but not quite a roast. Great to serve among friends.

PREPARATION TIME: 20 MINUTES
COOKING TIME: 35 MINUTES
SERVES: 4

4 chicken marylands
3 tbsp extra virgin olive oil
15–20 pearl onions (mixture of red and white), peeled, left whole
8 small carrots
12 whole button mushrooms
$2^1/_2$ cups dry white wine
8 cups chicken stock
2 sprigs fresh thyme, plus extra to serve
1 tbsp salted butter

1. Pat the chicken dry with paper towels. Season the marylands with salt and pepper and rub into the skin.
2. Heat the olive oil in a large heavy flameproof casserole dish over high heat. Sear the chicken on all sides then turn down the heat to medium and continue to cook for about 10 minutes, until lightly golden.
3. Add the vegetables and cook for a further 3 minutes. Be delicate when stirring because you don't want to tear the chicken skin.
4. Add the white wine and cover with a lid for about 5 minutes. Add half the chicken stock and continue to cook with the lid on for another 10 minutes.
5. Add the thyme, then turn down the heat again so it is at a light simmer. Leave for another 3 minutes. Remove the chicken drumsticks and vegetables from the cooking liquid and set aside.
6. In a frying pan, melt the butter on high heat and re-sear the chicken until it turns golden. Add the remaining chicken stock to the cooking liquid and bring to the boil. Season to taste.
7. Divide the chicken and vegetables between serving bowls. Ladle the hot stock over and garnish with extra thyme.

These juicy little numbers are quick, simple and always go down a treat.

Mediterranean lamb burgers

PREPARATION TIME: 35 MINUTES
COOKING TIME: APPROXIMATELY 10 MINUTES
SERVES: 6

6 Turkish bread rolls (or any bread you prefer)
olive oil, to brush

Tzatziki:

1 cup Greek yoghurt
$^3/_4$ cup finely diced Lebanese cucumber
2 garlic cloves, crushed
pinch each of sea salt and ground pepper, or to taste
$^1/_2$ lemon, juiced and grated
finely grated zest and juice of $^1/_2$ lemon

Patties:

600g lamb mince
$^1/_2$ red onion, diced
$^1/_2$ cup coriander, chopped
$^1/_2$ tsp freshly grated ginger (optional)
1–2 tbsp pine nuts
1 tsp crushed chili, or to taste
$^1/_2$ tsp salt and pepper
1 egg

For the salad:

2 cups baby spinach leaves
2 large tomatoes, sliced
1 red onion, sliced

1. For the tzatziki, combine all the ingredients in a bowl and refrigerate while you make the burgers.
2. To make the patties, mix all the ingredients together in a bowl and shape into 6 round patties of even thickness.
3. Cook the patties on a BBQ, chargrill or in a frying pan over medium-high heat for 3 minutes on each side.
4. Halve the Turkish bread rolls, brush with olive oil and lightly toast.
5. Place the patties onto the bottom half of each roll, then top with the salad and a big spoonful of tzatziki. Put the remaining roll halves on top, and serve.

Juicy gourmet beef burgers

PREPARATION TIME: 25 MINUTES
COOKING TIME: 20 MINUTES
SERVES: 6

1.2kg beef mince
1 egg
1 tbsp tomato sauce
pinch each of sea salt and cracked pepper
1 tbsp olive oil
2 brown onions, chopped
6 bacon rashers, rind removed, chopped
200g brie, cut into 6 slices
200g cheddar, cut into 6 slices
1 large avocado, sliced
6 sourdough buns, split and toasted

For the salad (inside the burger):

6 slices canned beetroot
2 cups rocket
3 Roma tomatoes, sliced
mustard, tomato or barbecue sauce, to taste

1. Combine the beef, egg, tomato sauce, sea salt and cracked pepper and roll into 6 balls. Halve each ball and flatten out to make 12 patties. Set aside.
2. Heat the olive oil in a large frying pan and cook the onion and bacon together until bacon pieces are crisp.
3. Spoon the mixture onto the centre of 6 patties. Place a slice of brie onto the onion mixture. Place the remaining patties on top and pinch the edges to seal.
4. Cook the patties on a BBQ, chargrill or in a frying pan over medium-high heat for 3 minutes on each side. When finished frying, lay a slice of cheddar on top of each patty to slightly melt with the heat.
5. Spread the sliced avocado inside the top half of the each bun and mash it slightly with a fork. Place the beef patty on the bottom half and top with salad. Add mustard, tomato or barbecue sauce to taste, and put the buns' tops on. Serve straight away.

Savoury impossible pie

A great dish to make when you can't be fussed making pastry. I found this old recipe in one of my mum's cookbooks from the 1960s. I've spiced it up a little, but it's still an excellent dish to serve a family.

PREPARATION TIME: 20 MINUTES
COOKING TIME: 35–40 MINUTES
SERVES: 5–6

3 eggs
2 cups milk
$^1/_2$ cup plain flour
1 tsp baking powder
125g salted butter, melted
400g can tuna, drained and flaked
1 onion, finely chopped
2 garlic cloves, crushed
1 cup grated vintage cheddar
$^1/_4$ cup grated parmesan
$^1/_4$ cup chopped flat-leaf parsley
paprika to dust, optional

1. Preheat the oven to 180°C and lightly grease a 23cm pie dish.
2. In a large bowl, beat together the eggs, milk, flour, baking powder and butter. Season with salt and freshly ground black pepper.
3. Stir in the remaining ingredients (except paprika). Pour the mixture into the prepared dish. Dust with paprika (if using) and bake for 35–40 minutes, or until set.
4. Serve hot or cold.

Meat pie

Traditional pie pastry on the bottom, slow-cooked beef in the middle topped with puff pastry and truffle mash make this an absolute winner.

PREPARATION TIME: 40 MINUTES
COOKING TIME: 2 HOURS 45 MINUTES
SERVES: 8

¹/₄ tsp pepper
¹/₄ tsp chilli powder
1kg beef brisket or rump steak, cut into 1cm cubes
1 tbsp salted butter
1 brown onion, thinly sliced
6 button mushrooms, thinly sliced
1 garlic clove, crushed
300ml pale ale
¹/₂ cup barbecue sauce
2 teaspoons Worcestershire sauce (optional)
400ml beef stock
2 sprigs fresh thyme
1 bay leaf
2 tsp cornflour
2 x quantity Savoury Non-Shrink Pastry (page 44), uncooked, in a 23cm pie dish
1 sheet puff pastry
Truffle Mash, to serve (page 102)

1. Preheat the oven to 150°C. Sprinkle the pepper and chilli powder over the beef.

2. Melt the butter in a deep flameproof casserole dish. Fry the onion, mushrooms and garlic until the onion is slightly transparent. Remove from the dish and set aside.

3. Cook the beef in several batches for 1–2 minutes per batch, turning to seal and brown. Return all the meat, onion and mushrooms to the dish. Add the ale, barbecue sauce, Worcestershire sauce (if using), beef stock, thyme and bay leaf.

4. Combine the cornflour with 2 tsp water in a small bowl until smooth, then stir into the pan. Bring to a simmer, cover, then place into the oven for about 2 hours or until the meat is really tender.

5. Transfer to a bowl and cool completely before spooning into the pastry shell (this way you won't have to blind bake pastry). Increase oven to 220°C. Top pie with puff pastry and press edges to seal. Make a few little slits in the centre of the pie to allow steam to escape.

6. Bake pie for about 35 minutes or until pastry has risen and turned a nice golden colour. To serve, top with mash.

   NOTE: For a more golden finish, if not topping with truffle mash, beat one egg and brush the top of the puff pastry prior to cooking.

Shredded beef

This is a great recipe to have handy because it can be used for many different recipes: meat pie, lasagne, ravioli – any kind of pasta, really – burritos, tacos . . . many wonderful dishes.

This is an old recipe handed down through the Pesutto family, and was given to me by my agent, Chelsea.

PREPARATION TIME: 10 MINUTES
COOKING TIME: 1½–2 HOURS
SERVES: 10+

2kg diced lean beef shoulder
2 x 400g cans organic diced tomatoes
1 tbsp tomato paste (or to taste)
4 garlic cloves, chopped
2 cups beef stock
1 tbsp dried oregano
½ cup vinegar
1–2 tsp salt (or to taste)

1. Place all ingredients in a large pot, and top up with some water if necessary, to fully cover the meat.
2. Bring to the boil, then reduce the heat and simmer for about 1½–2 hours, stirring every 15 minutes until the meat falls apart and the liquid has reduced. It should still be wet, not boiled off completely.
3. This can be frozen in portions to use as required.

Pork spare ribs

This is my mother's recipe. During my vegetarian phase this was by far the dish I missed most.

It's surprisingly easy and very juicy. I usually stir-fry some Asian greens to complement it.

PREPARATION TIME: 10 MINUTES + MARINATING
COOKING TIME: 40 MINUTES
SERVES: 5

3–4 tbsp soy sauce
1 tbsp brown sugar or honey
1 tbsp lemon juice
1 tsp crushed garlic
2 tsp tomato sauce
1kg pork spare ribs

1. Combine all the ingredients (except the ribs) in a jar and shake well. Place the ribs into a shallow dish and pour the liquid over, making sure they are evenly covered.
2. Cover, place into the fridge and marinate for a few hours.
3. Preheat the oven to 180°C. Transfer the ribs to a large baking tray, evenly spaced, and cook for 40 minutes. Serve immediately.

This is mouth-watering. The pork is tender and juicy without having to brine it, making this both easy and delicious.

Roasted rack of pork with fennel and maple

PREPARATION TIME: 15 MINUTES
COOKING TIME: 45 MINUTES + RESTING
SERVES: 4

2 tbsp fresh rosemary
1 garlic clove
2 tsp fennel seeds
1 tsp dried chilli flakes
2 tsp sea salt
2 tbsp olive oil
2 tbsp maple syrup
1kg pork rack

1. Preheat the oven to 220°C and line a baking dish with baking paper.
2. Using a mortar and pestle, grind the rosemary, garlic, fennel, chilli and sea salt together until well combined.
3. Combine the mixture with the olive oil and 1 tbsp of the maple syrup. Rub into the pork really well. Place into the dish and roast for 35 minutes. Turn the temperature down to 180°C, coat the pork rack with remaining maple syrup and roast for another 10 minutes.
4. Remove the pork from the oven, cover loosely with foil and let rest for 10–15 minutes. Slice into cutlets and serve with apple sauce (see below).

Apple sauce

PREPARATION TIME: 10 MINUTES
COOKING TIME: 15–20 MINUTES
SERVES: 4

4 granny smith apples, peeled, cored and chopped
3/4 cup caster sugar
1/4 cup apple cider vinegar
1 tsp salt
1 cinnamon stick

Combine apples, sugar, vinegar, salt, cinnamon stick and 1/2 cup water in a saucepan. Cover and cook over medium heat for 15–20 minutes, or until apples are soft. Allow to cool then mash with a fork or puree in a blender.

The non-shrink pastry crust

A lot of pastry crusts have a habit of shrinking while they are being cooked. You can help avoid this problem by refrigerating the dough before baking and also over-hanging the pastry a little when blind baking, but here I've got an easy recipe that hardly ever shrinks.

This recipe can be used for a sweet or savoury pastry. If you want to use it for a pie with a top, just double the recipe.

PREPARATION TIME: 15 MINUTES
COOKING TIME: 25 MINUTES
MAKES: 23CM PIE OR TART SHELL

115g butter
$1^3/_4$ cups plain flour
(for a sweet pastry add $1^1/_4$ tbsp caster sugar)

1. Preheat the oven to 170°C and grease a 23cm pie dish or loose-bottomed tart tin.
2. Melt the butter in a large saucepan, then remove from heat and sift the flour into the melted butter.
3. For a sweet pastry, sift the caster sugar into the mixture.
4. Turn the dough out onto a floured surface and knead until smooth and elastic. Roll out between 2 sheets of baking paper.
5. Line the tin with the dough, pressing into the edges. If pastry breaks, just press bits into bare areas.
6. To blind bake, cover the pastry with a sheet of baking paper and fill with pie weights or uncooked rice. Bake for 15 minutes, then remove the paper and weights and cook a further 8–10 minutes, until the pastry is dry and lightly golden. Remove from the oven and set aside to cool.
7. Alternatively, if you do not have pie weights you can freeze the pastry for 15 minutes prior to baking and using a fork, gently prick the base of the pastry shell before placing in the oven.
8. Fill with ingredients for the pie or tart.

Classic sweet pastry

Growing up I would constantly make pastry for lemon meringue pies and mulberry tarts. I remember my grandma watching me one day and telling me to 'stop overworking' the pastry, but at that age my little cold hands made excellent pastry as I never overworked the dough.

Pastry can be very easy but also frustrating at times. The older I got the more I seemed to overwork the dough, producing crusts with too much elasticity. So I developed a foolproof pastry recipe that is quick and easy. Even though pastry connoisseurs might scoff at using a food processor, it minimises the time spent kneading and keeps the pastry cool, away from hot hands (which will melt the butter too fast), producing a softer more crumbly crust, which is exactly want you want.

PREPARATION TIME: 15 MINUTES + 30 MINUTES CHILLING
COOKING TIME: 20 MINUTES
MAKES: 23CM PIE OR TART SHELL

2 cups plain flour
150g cold butter, chopped
1 1/2 tbsp icing sugar
2 small egg yolks
1/2 tsp finely grated lemon zest
1/2 tsp vanilla essence

1. Place all the ingredients into a food processor and, using the pulse button, process in short bursts until it starts to bind. Pour out the mixture onto a floured surface. Knead briefly and make into a ball, cover the ball in cling film and let rest in the fridge for 15 minutes.

2. Return the dough to the floured surface and press out flat, then roll out to fit a 23cm loose-bottomed tart tin. The pastry is delicate so use a light touch.

3. Press the pastry into the tart tin, making sure all the cracks have been sealed with your fingers. Place in the freezer for 15 minutes. Preheat the oven to 200°C.

4. Lightly prick the pastry with a fork a few times and bake for 5 minutes, then reduce the temperature to 175°C and cook a further 15 minutes.

5. If you're keeping the pastry overnight or worried the filling might seep into it, you can seal it with an egg white wash. Let the pastry cool for 3–5 minutes then brush the pastry lightly with beaten egg white.

NOTE: If you are not using a food processor, sift the flour and icing sugar into a bowl. Add the butter and use your fingertips to rub it into the flour until it resembles breadcrumbs. In a separate bowl, combine the egg, lemon zest, vanilla and water. Pour into flour mixture and mix with a fork lightly until combined.

250g butter, chopped and
    softened
1 cup brown sugar
3/4 cup caster sugar
2 eggs
1 tsp vanilla extract
3 1/2 cups self-raising flour
2 cups good quality milk
    chocolate chips (I use
    Cadbury)
1 1/2 cups dark chocolate chips
    (60% cocoa)

The ultimate chocolate chip cookies

I love these cookies! Whenever I make them they seem to disappear before they've even cooled down. The trick is to add two types of chocolate chips. This gives them an incredible richness. They're extra chunky, too – just the way I like my choc chip cookies.

PREPARATION TIME: 20 MINUTES
BAKING TIME: 10–15 MINUTES
MAKES: 20–25 (MAY VARY DEPENDING ON SIZE)

1. Preheat the oven to 160°C and grease 2 large baking trays.
2. Use an electric mixer to cream the butter and sugars until light and fluffy. Beat in the eggs and vanilla.
3. Stir in the flour, then fold the chocolate chips through the mixture.
4. Using your hands, grab small amounts and roll into balls, then place onto the prepared trays and press to flatten.
5. Bake for 10–15 minutes or until golden and risen slightly. Leave on the trays for a couple of minutes – they will firm up as they cool. Transfer to a wire rack to cool completely (though they might get snatched up before then).

NOTE: If you like your cookies thinner and more crisp, use 1/2 cup less flour.

Anzac biscuits

PREPARATION TIME: 15 MINUTES
COOKING TIME: 15 MINUTES
MAKES: 10–15

2 cups plain flour
2 tsp bicarb soda
2 cups rolled oats
2 cups desiccated coconut
1 cup brown sugar
300g butter, chopped
$\frac{1}{2}$ cup golden syrup

1. Preheat the oven to 180°C and line 2 baking trays with baking paper.
2. Sift the flour and bicarb soda into a mixing bowl. Stir in the oats, coconut and sugar and make a well in the centre.
3. Melt the butter and golden syrup together, and pour into the flour mixture. Mix with a wooden spoon until evenly combined. Roll tablespoons of the mixture into balls and place about 4cm apart onto the trays.
4. Press the dough down lightly – they flatten out quite a lot while baking and I prefer mine more chunky.
5. Bake for 15 minutes, until nice and golden. Leave on the trays to cool until firm, and then transfer to a wire rack to cool completely. Store in an airtight container for up to 1 week.

Apricot & sultana rock cakes

A name to match the look, 'Rock Cakes' were once a popular treat in Great Britain. As they use less egg than traditional cakes, they were good to make during war times. I love the texture – it's sweet and crumbly and more like a scone than a biscuit. Growing up I would often buy these from the local bakery but nothing beats making them yourself and eating them fresh from the oven.

PREPARATION TIME: 15 MINUTES
COOKING TIME: 10–15 MINUTES
MAKES: ABOUT 5

2 cups self-raising flour
$^1/_2$ tsp ground ginger
80g cold salted butter, cubed
$^1/_2$ cup sugar
$^1/_3$ cup sultanas (add more if desired)
$^1/_3$ cup chopped dried apricots
1 egg
$^1/_4$ cup milk
$^1/_2$ tsp vanilla extract
caster sugar, to sprinkle

1. Preheat the oven to 200°C and lightly grease a baking tray.
2. Sift the flour and ginger into a bowl and add the butter. Use your fingertips to lightly rub together until evenly combined (it will look a little like breadcrumbs). Stir in the sugar, sultanas and apricots, and make a well in the centre.
3. Whisk the egg, milk and vanilla with a fork until combined. Add to the dry ingredients and mix with a wooden spoon to a stiff dough.
4. Spoon the mixture into 5 heaps on the prepared tray, leaving about 4cm space in between. Bake for 10–15 minutes, until golden. While still hot, sprinkle with sugar. Transfer to a wire rack to cool.

Since moving to New York, one of the things I miss most from Australia is this special treat.

Cherry Ripe slice

The unfortunate fact is that Cherry Ripe only exists in Australia! So when I want my Cherry Ripe fix, I make this slice, which is reminiscent of the slice my Aunty Kim makes for Christmas every year. It's a heartwarming dessert to get you through the difficult days if you live abroad.

PREPARATION TIME: 50 MINUTES
COOKING TIME: 45 MINUTES
MAKES: 15–20 SQUARES

Base:

1$\frac{1}{2}$ cups plain flour
3 tbsp Dutch (dark) cocoa powder
$\frac{3}{4}$ cup caster sugar
$\frac{1}{2}$ tsp baking powder
100g salted butter, chopped and softened
50ml cold milk

Cherry filling:

600g glacé cherries
125g condensed milk
150g desiccated coconut
1 tsp vanilla extract

Topping:

400g dark chocolate, chopped

1. Preheat the oven to 180°C and line an 18cm square cake tin with baking paper.
2. To make the base, put the flour, cocoa, sugar and baking powder in a bowl and rub in the butter until it's utterly worked through and all the lumps have gone. Add the milk and mix to a soft dough.
3. Press into the base of the tin firmly and evenly. Bake for 15–20 minutes or until set and dry on top. Remove from the oven and leave to cool.
4. To make the filling, put the cherries into a food processor, and process until very finely chopped. (This can be done by hand if you have the patience and don't mind the stickiness.) Mix in the condensed milk, coconut and vanilla until you have a smooth, pink, coconut paste. Spread evenly over the chocolate base. Return to the oven and bake for a further 25 minutes. Remove from the oven and leave until cold.
5. For the topping, melt the dark chocolate (I prefer to melt the chocolate the traditional way, in a bowl over simmering water on a stovetop) and spread over the top. Leave to set.
6. Cut into bars, then refrigerate. The chocolate will become quite hard in the fridge, so it's better to slice first.

3 cups plain flour

4 tsp baking powder

1 tsp ground cinnamon

1 cup caster sugar

$^2/_3$ cup milk

$^1/_2$ cup canola or similar
  vegetable oil

2 eggs

$1^1/_2$ tbsp honey

2 tsp vanilla extract

2 pears, peeled, cored and
  finely diced

2 ripe bananas, finely chopped

Spiced pear and banana muffins

PREPARATION TIME: 20 MINUTES
COOKING TIME: 25 MINUTES
MAKES: 12

1. Preheat the oven to 190°C. Line a 12-hole muffin tin with paper cases.
2. Sift the flour, baking powder, cinnamon and sugar into a mixing bowl and make a well in the centre.
3. In a separate bowl, whisk the milk, oil, eggs, honey and vanilla. Slowly combine the mixtures together until just combined (do not over-mix), then fold through the pear and banana.
4. Fill the muffin tins so that they are just over $^3/_4$ full. This will give you a nice round top at the end.
5. Bake for 25 minutes. If you are serving hot, drizzle some extra honey over the top of the muffins.

Banana Nutella bread with choc chips

PREPARATION TIME: 25 MINUTES
COOKING TIME: 55–60 MINUTES
SERVES: 8–10

1. Preheat the oven to 175°C, and line a 23 x 12cm loaf pan with baking paper.

2. Using an electric mixer, beat the butter and both sugars together until combined. Add the eggs and vanilla and beat until well blended. Reduce the speed to low and add the milk, banana and vegetable oil.

3. Slowly add the flour and bicarb soda, and mix until just combined – don't overbeat. Stir in the chocolate chips.

4. Spoon half the mixture into the loaf tin, drop spoonfuls of the Nutella on top, then add the remaining batter. Using a knife, swirl the Nutella through the batter.

5. Bake for 55–60 minutes, until golden brown and firm to a gentle touch in the centre. Don't overcook it as it will become dry. Cool in the tin for 10–15 minutes, then turn out onto a wire rack to cool.

60g salted butter, softened

$^3/_4$ cup caster sugar

1 tbsp brown sugar

2 eggs

1 tsp vanilla extract

$^1/_3$ cup milk

1 cup mashed ripe bananas

3 teaspoons vegetable oil

2 cups plain flour

$^3/_4$ tsp bicarb soda

$^3/_4$ cup dark chocolate chips

$^1/_2$ cup Nutella

Cherry crumble

This is such an easy dish to serve. You can use fresh cherries if you don't mind the extra time spent pitting them.

PREPARATION TIME: 25 MINUTES
COOKING TIME: 20–25 MINUTES
SERVES: 4

Crumble:

melted butter and a little flour, to prepare ramekins
250g salted butter, chopped
1¼ cups rolled oats
2¼ cups plain flour
1 cup packed brown sugar

Cherry filling:

800g canned, frozen or fresh cherries, pitted
2 tbsp caster sugar
1 tsp cornflour

1. Preheat the oven to 190°C. Grease four 300ml ramekins with the melted butter. Dust with flour, shaking out the excess.
2. Melt the butter in a saucepan, then remove from the heat. Stir in the oats, flour and brown sugar. A crumbly dough will form. Press some of the mixture into each ramekin so it is about one quarter full.
3. To make the cherry filling, place the cherries in a saucepan with the caster sugar. Stir over medium heat until the sugar has dissolved, then increase the heat and bring to the boil. Mix the cornflour in a small bowl with 1 teaspoon of water until smooth. Stir into the cherry mixture and return to the boil.
4. Spoon the mixture into the ramekins over the crust until almost full. Sprinkle the remaining crumble mixture over the cherries. Bake for 20–25 minutes, or until the top is slightly golden.

Lamingtons

This traditional Aussie/Kiwi number is so delicious that it's my mum's favourite dessert. I often make these for my American friends since it's not something that can be found in bakeries over there.

The sponge is the most crucial part to a great lamington.

PREPARATION TIME: 40 MINUTES + COOLING
COOKING TIME: 30 MINUTES
MAKES: 8 (MAY VARY DEPENDING ON SIZE)

Sponge:

125g salted butter, chopped and softened
1¼ cups caster sugar
1 tsp vanilla extract
3 eggs
1 tbsp canola oil
1 tbsp sour cream
1¾ cups self-raising flour, sifted
½ cup milk

Icing:

1 tbsp salted butter
200g good quality dark chocolate, chopped (avoid cooking chocolate)
2 cups icing sugar
1 tbsp Dutch (dark) cocoa powder
2 cups desiccated coconut

1. Preheat the oven to 180°C. Grease a 28 x 20cm tin and line with baking paper.
2. Using an electric mixer, beat the butter and sugar together until light and fluffy. Beat in the vanilla. Add the eggs one at a time, while beating continuously. Add the oil and sour cream and beat until combined.
3. Turn down the mixer to low and add half the flour and half the milk. Mix until combined then add the rest of the flour and milk and mix to combine.
4. Pour the mixture into the prepared tin and bake for 30 minutes. To test whether the cake is ready, insert a skewer in the middle of the cake. If the skewer comes out clean, you can remove from the oven.

5. Cool in the tin for a few minutes before turning out onto a wire rack, then place a tea towel on top of the cake to prevent drying out. Set aside to cool completely.

6. To make the icing, melt the butter and chocolate together in a saucepan over low heat. Remove from the heat.

7. Sift the icing sugar and cocoa together, and gradually add to the chocolate, stirring until combined. If the mixture is too thick, you can add a little bit of hot water.

8. Cut the cake into squares of your preferred size. Scatter a layer of coconut over a plate. Dip a cake square into the icing, then transfer to the plate and roll in coconut until it is covered. Place onto a large plate.

9. Refrigerate for at least 20 minutes before serving. This goes down a treat with a hot cup of coffee.

225g can sliced beetroot, drained
1 cup almond milk
1 tsp white vinegar
1 cup white sugar
$1/4$ cup canola oil
1 tsp vanilla extract
$1^{1}/4$ cup plain flour
$1/2$ cup Dutch (dark) cocoa powder
1 tsp bicarb soda
$3/4$ tsp baking powder

Vegan chocolate cupcakes

PREPARATION TIME: 30 MINUTES
COOKING TIME: 20 MINUTES
MAKES: 12

1. Preheat the oven to 190°C and line a 12-cupcake tin with paper cases.
2. Puree the beetroot using a food processor or a stick blender (you'll need $1/4$ cup beetroot puree).
3. Combine the almond milk and vinegar in a large bowl. Mix well and stand for 2 minutes (the milk will curdle slightly).
4. Add the sugar, beetroot, oil and vanilla, then sift the flour, cocoa powder, bicarb soda and baking powder over. Beat with a handheld electric mixer for 1–2 minutes, until smooth. Fill the cupcake cases to about $3/4$ full.
5. Bake for 20 minutes. Using a cake tester or skewer, check that the cupcakes are ready, then remove. If the skewer or tester comes out clean, the cupcakes are done.
6. You can serve this with a dusting of cocoa powder or icing sugar; however, this cupcake is quite rich already.

Chocolate self-saucing pudding

This recipe is great because I usually have most of the ingredients in the pantry ready to go. A cool serving suggestion is to put it into coffee mugs. That way you can just pass them around in individual servings.

PREPARATION TIME 30 MINUTES
COOKING TIME: 30 MINUTES
SERVES: 4

1. Preheat the oven to 180°C.
2. For the pudding, sift the flour, cocoa and sugars together. In a separate bowl combine the egg, butter, milk and vanilla and add to dry ingredients. Stir until just combined, but take care not to over-mix. Pour the batter into a 5–6 cup capacity ovenproof dish, and stand on a baking tray.
3. To make the sauce, place the dark chocolate and milk into a saucepan and stir over low heat until chocolate has melted. Bring to the boil, then gently pour the sauce over the pudding mixture. The chocolate sauce should completely cover the pudding.
4. Bake for 30 minutes, until the pudding is firm to touch. Serve immediately with ice-cream or cream.

Pudding:

3/4 cup self-raising flour
3 tbsp cocoa powder
1/4 cup caster sugar
1 tbsp brown sugar
1 egg, lightly beaten
1 1/2 tbsp salted butter, melted
1/2 cup milk
1/2 tsp vanilla extract

Chocolate sauce:

150g dark chocolate, broken up
1 1/2 cups milk

Chocolate mud cake

This baby is decadent and rich, and it makes an excellent dessert for a suave dinner party.

PREPARATION TIME: 30 MINUTES
COOKING TIME: 1 HOUR 20 MINUTES
SERVES: 10

250g butter, chopped
300g dark chocolate, chopped
$2\frac{1}{4}$ cups caster sugar
2 eggs, lightly beaten
$1\frac{1}{4}$ cup self-raising flour
$1\frac{1}{4}$ cups plain flour
$\frac{1}{4}$ cup cocoa powder

Chocolate ganache topping:

400g dark chocolate, chopped
1 cup thickened cream
1 tbsp cocoa powder

1. Preheat the oven to 180°C. Grease a 22cm round cake tin and line the base with baking paper.
2. In a saucepan melt the butter and chocolate over low heat. Add the sugar and 1 cup cold water, and stir until smooth. Set aside to cool for 10 minutes then transfer to a large mixing bowl.
3. Add the eggs and stir to combine. Sift the flours and cocoa powder over, then stir until smooth. Pour mixture into the prepared pan. Bake for 1 hour and 10 minutes, or until firm to a gentle touch in the centre. Stand for 10 minutes in the tin, then turn out onto a wire rack to cool.
4. To make the chocolate ganache topping, melt the chocolate and cream together in a small saucepan over low heat, stirring until smooth. Add the cocoa and stir through. Place the saucepan in the fridge for 20–30 minutes, until the mixture is thick enough to spread. Spread over the entire cake. Let it sit for 10 minutes before serving.

NOTE: The ganache topping makes a little more than you will need. I store it in an airtight container in the fridge to serve over ice-cream.

Quick chocolate cake

This chocolate cake is quick and easy and always popular. My mum used to make this cake for my sisters' and my birthdays every year. She would decorate them to look like monsters, using all my favourite lollies. This is a good cake for decorating as it's easy to cut into shapes.

PREPARATION TIME: 10 MINUTES
COOKING TIME: 25–35 MINUTES
SERVES: 8

3 cups self-raising flour
$1^1/_4$ cups white sugar
3 tbsp cocoa powder
$^1/_2$ tsp bicarb soda
1 cup milk
2 eggs
1 tsp vanilla extract
125g butter, melted

1. Preheat oven to 180°C. Grease two 20cm (base measurement) round cake tins and line the bases with baking paper. Sift the dry ingredients into a large mixing bowl and make a well in the centre.
2. Whisk the milk, eggs and vanilla in another bowl. Add to the dry ingredients along with the butter. Use an electric mixer to beat for 1 minute or until well combined. Divide between prepared tins and bake for 25 minutes or until a skewer comes out clean when inserted into the middle of a cake.
3. Cool completely before icing with your favourite icing.

NOTE: This recipe is great because you can use a variety of cake tins. For one large rectangular cake I'd recommend a 32 x 23cm cake tin. Cook for 35 minutes.

A simple icing recipe I like to use:

Melt 20g of butter in a saucepan. Remove from heat and add 1 cup sifted icing sugar, $^1/_2$ teaspoon of lemon juice, 1 tablespoon Dutch cocoa powder, and 1–3 tablespoons milk, depending on how thick you want it. Mix well. When icing the cake use a knife and have a cup of hot water handy. While icing just dip the knife into the hot water now and then so the icing spreads easily.
I sometimes sprinkle shredded coconut on top.

NOTE: You can sandwich the two cakes together with icing, or serve as two separate cakes.

Berry pavlova

An iconic Aussie classic. This is always a great dish to serve to foreign friends as visually it is so unique and, luckily, tastes as good as it looks.

PREPARATION TIME: 30 MINUTES
COOKING TIME: 1 HOUR + COOLING
SERVES: 8

8 egg whites
2 cups caster sugar, sifted
1 tbsp cornflour
2 tsp white vinegar

Topping:

300ml thickened cream
1 tbsp icing sugar
1 tsp vanilla extract
250g strawberries, hulled and sliced
150g raspberries
150g blueberries

1. Preheat the oven to 150°C and line a large baking tray with baking paper (a round pizza tray is ideal).
2. Before mixing, wipe all bowls and utensils with white vinegar as any trace of grease will prevent the egg whites beating up to a good volume.
3. Using an electric mixer, beat the egg whites until stiff peaks form. Add the caster sugar, cornflour and vinegar gradually and beat for another 3–5 minutes, or until you can no longer feel the grains of sugar between your fingers.
4. Spoon the mixture onto the prepared tray. Using a knife or spatula, shape into a circle at your preferred height (as this doesn't rise). Leave a little room around the edge as it will spread slightly.
5. Bake for 1 hour (if too much browning occurs on top just carefully place some foil lightly over). When done, switch off the oven and open the oven door slightly. Leave the pavlova in the oven to cool.
6. For the topping, use an electric mixer to beat the cream, icing sugar and vanilla until soft peaks form. Place pavlova on a serving plate and top with the cream mixture and berries.

NOTE: To make a berry sauce, heat the berries with some sugar in a saucepan until slightly thickened, then cool and use to top pavlova.

Custard tart

PREPARATION TIME: 30 MINUTES + 30 MINUTES CHILLING
COOKING TIME: 40–45 MINUTES
SERVES: 6–8

Pastry:
1 quantity Classic Sweet Pastry (page 45), blind baked and cooled

Custard filling:
1¼ cups milk
3 eggs
¼ cup caster sugar
2 tsp vanilla extract
a sprinkle of nutmeg

rasperries and icing sugar, to serve, optional

1. For the custard filling, pour the milk into a saucepan and heat over low heat until warm. Remove from the heat, add the eggs, sugar and vanilla and whisk together.
2. Pour the filling into the prepared pastry shell so that it is just less than completely full (you may have a little left over). I like to place the pastry shell in the oven before I pour the mixture in, as it can be tricky to carry. Sprinkle some nutmeg over the custard tart, then bake for 20-25 minutes, or until set.
3. Once the pie has cooled, you might like to top with raspberries and a sprinkle of icing sugar.

Mulberry tart

Mulberry tart is the dish that my family demands of me the most. It became our annual tart dish as mulberries are very seasonal and fragile. My sisters and I would sneak into a deserted paddock which was filled with the most amazing mulberry trees. We would only have to shake the tree to have bucket loads of the ripest, freshest mulberries. Our mum saw how much we loved them and decided she would plant a mulberry tree for us in our backyard. I go back even today and continue to cook that mulberry tart, fighting off fruit bats to obtain the last few berries of the season!

PREPARATION TIME: 15 MINUTES
COOKING TIME: 25 MINUTES
SERVES: 8

1 quantity Classic Sweet Pastry (page 45), cooked and cooled

Filling:

3–4 cups of fresh or frozen mulberries (or berries of your choice)
1 cup white sugar
2 teaspoons cornflour

1. Preheat the oven to 180°C.
2. Heat the berries in a saucepan with the sugar and a teaspoon of water (the berries have plenty of juice, but this will make sure nothing burns on the bottom of the saucepan). Stir over medium-low heat until the sugar has dissolved, then bring slowly to the boil.
3. Combine the cornflour with 2 teaspoons of water in a small bowl until smooth, then stir into the berry mixture. Cook until thickened.
4. Remove from heat then cool before adding to the pastry shell. Bake for 20 minutes, or until set.

Mince pies

I have a weak spot for mince pies, and when Christmas time rolls around it's never the same without them. Traditionally, this is an English recipe but of course, it's much loved in Australia.

PREPARATION TIME: 30 MINUTES + 30 MINUTES CHILLING
COOKING TIME: ABOUT 1 HOUR
MAKES: ABOUT 16

Pastry:

450g cold salted butter, cubed
700g plain flour
200g caster sugar
1 egg, beaten, to glaze

Filling:

225g sultanas
225g currants
125g candied mixed peel
100g glacé cherries, chopped
125g butter, chopped
175g raw sugar
1 tsp ground cinnamon
$1/2$ tsp mixed spice
finely grated zest and juice of 1 orange
$1/4$ cup brandy

1. To make the pastry, use your fingertips to rub the butter into the flour, then stir in the sugar.
2. Gather the dough into a ball. This is a very delicate pastry, so it may be a little tricky to handle. Wrap in cling wrap and refrigerate for 30 minutes.
3. To make the filling, combine all ingredients in a saucepan, bring to the boil, then reduce the heat to low and simmer for 30 minutes. Cool before using, or keep in airtight container or jars in the fridge if making ahead of time.

   TO MAKE THE PIES:
4. Preheat the oven to 180°C. Grease mince pie tins or muffin tins with butter, then dust with flour.
5. Using your hands, take about a tablespoon of the pastry (depending on the tin size) and press into the tin. Spoon the fruit mixture into the pastry cups.
6. Make the lids by rolling up a small bit of pastry and pressing it between your hands to flatten it out. Gently place onto the pie and press the edges to seal. Brush the tops of the pies with the egg.
7. Bake for 20–30 minutes or until golden, then cool on a rack. Dust with icing sugar.

Decadence to die for.

Nutella soufflé

This was a recipe featured on my food blog in the very beginning.
I remember baking it after work in my old Brooklyn apartment (with a
terrible oven). I had to rush to get the photo taken as the sun was going
down. It is still one of my favourite blog entries.

PREPARATION TIME: 25 MINUTES + 30 MINUTES CHILLING
COOKING TIME: 30 MINUTES
SERVES: 6

6 tbsp Nutella
$1/2$ cup plain flour
$1/2$ cup cocoa powder
$1/2$ tsp baking powder
160g unsalted butter
140g cup good quality chocolate (40–70% cocoa), broken up
4 eggs
1 tsp vanilla extract
1 cup sugar

1. Preheat the oven to 175°C. Grease six $3/4$ cup capacity ramekins or souffle dishes.

2. Place 6 tablespoons of Nutella onto a tray lined with baking paper and put into the freezer for 30 minutes. This will help keep the Nutella firm so it stays in the centre of the soufflé while it cooks.

3. Sift the flour, cocoa and baking powder into a bowl and set aside.

4. Melt the butter in a small saucepan over low heat, and then add chocolate. Stir until the chocolate is completely melted, and remove from the heat.

5. Using an electric mixer on medium–high speed, beat the eggs, vanilla, sugar and a pinch of salt in a large bowl for about 5 minutes, until it turns a soft, pale yellow. Beat in the chocolate mixture, then stir in the flour mixture.

6. Spoon half the batter into the prepared ramekins. Drop 1 tablespoon of the chilled Nutella into the centre of each, then cover with remaining batter.

7. Place a roasting pan in the oven and fill $1/3$ of the way with water. Stand the ramekins in the roasting pan. Bake for about 30 minutes, until well risen. Cool for 5 minutes and serve warm.

Lemon meringue pie

I used to make this for my grandma all the time; she absolutely loves this pie.

PREPARATION TIME: 30 MINUTES
COOKING TIME: 15–20 MINUTES
SERVES: 8

1 quantity Classic Sweet Pastry (page 45), cooked and cooled

Filling:
1$\frac{1}{4}$ cup white sugar
3 tbsp plain flour
4$\frac{1}{2}$ tbsp cornflour
finely grated zest and juice of 4 lemons
3 tbsp salted butter
6 egg yolks, beaten (keep the egg whites separate for the meringue)

Meringue topping:
6 egg whites
3 tbsp white sugar
2 tbsp icing sugar
1–2 tbsp cornflour (2 tbsp will give a crispier finish)

1. To make the filling, whisk 1 cup of the sugar, the flour and cornflour in a medium saucepan. Stir in the lemon juice and zest, and 2$\frac{1}{4}$ cups water. Cook over medium-high heat, stirring frequently until the mixture comes to the boil. Add the butter and continue to stir until melted and smooth.
2. Remove from heat and mix in the egg yolks quickly. Replace on the heat and return to the boil. Continue to cook, stirring constantly, until the filling has thickened. Remove from the heat and pour into the pastry shell.
3. To make the topping, use an electric mixer to beat the egg whites until soft peaks form. In a separate bowl sift the sugars and cornflour together. Slowly add to the egg whites while beating. (The best way to tell if the meringue is ready is to flip the bowl upside down. If it is done, the meringue won't move.) Using a spatula, spread the meringue on top of the lemon filling until it forms quite a large mound.
4. Bake for 5–10 minutes, until the meringue peaks start to brown slightly on top.

Hot cross buns

PREPARATION TIME: 30 MINUTES + 1 HOUR 45 MINUTES RISING
COOKING TIME: 25 MINUTES
MAKES: 12

1/2 cup lukewarm milk
1/3 cup caster sugar
7g sachet dry yeast (2 tsp)
2 1/2 cups plain flour
2 tsp mixed spice
2 tsp ground cinnamon
1/4 tsp ground nutmeg
50g chilled butter, chopped
1 egg, lightly beaten
1 1/2 cup sultanas (you can replace sultanas with chocolate chips if you prefer)
1 tbsp apricot jam, warmed

Flour paste:
1/2 cup plain flour
1 tbsp sugar

1. Place the milk, sugar and yeast in a bowl and stir until combined. Cover and place in a warm area for 10 minutes or until it looks foamy.

2. Meanwhile, sift the flour and spices into a large mixing bowl. Add the butter and rub in with your fingers until the mixture resembles breadcrumbs. Make a well in the centre.

3. Add the yeast mixture, egg, sultanas and 1/4 cup warm water. Using a wooden spoon, stir until evenly combined. Cover and set aside in a warm place for 1 hour or until doubled in size.

4. Preheat the oven to 200°C and line a 28 x 18cm baking tray with baking paper. Turn dough onto a floured surface and knead for 5 to 8 minutes or until smooth. Divide the mixture evenly into 12 portions and roll into balls. Place the balls onto the prepared tray a little bit apart (they will double in size). Cover and set aside in a warm place for 45 minutes.

5. To make the flour paste, whisk the flour, sugar and 1/3 cup cold water together until smooth. Pour mixture into a piping bag fitted with a small nozzle and pipe crosses onto the buns. (I pipe buns all at once with long lines to make it quicker.)

6. Bake buns for 10 minutes. Reduce oven temperature to 180°C and bake a further 15 minutes or until golden and cooked through. Remove from the oven and brush apricot jam over the warm buns. Transfer to a wire rack to cool.

Sweet scones

PREPARATION TIME: 15 MINUTES
COOKING TIME: 10–12 MINUTES
MAKES: ABOUT 10

2 cups self-raising flour
1/4 cup caster sugar
1/2 cup thick cream
1/2 cup lemonade
1/2 cup sultanas (optional)
2 tbsp milk
cream and jam, to serve

1. Preheat the oven to 220°C. Line a baking tray with baking paper.
2. Sift the flour and sugar together into a bowl. Add the cream, lemonade and sultanas (if using). Mix with a knife to form a soft dough.
3. Gently turn out onto a lightly floured bench and knead very lightly until combined. Pat out to 2.5cm thick. Using a 6cm scone cutter or a glass, cut out scones and place onto the prepared baking tray.
4. Brush the milk over the top of each scone and bake for 10–12 minutes, until risen and golden brown. Serve hot with cream and your favourite jam.

Notes

Savoury scones

PREPARATION TIME: 15 MINUTES
COOKING TIME: 10–12 MINUTES
MAKES ABOUT: 10

3 cups self-raising flour
$^1/_4$ tsp salt
1 cup cream
1 cup lemonade
1 egg
1 tbsp milk

1. Preheat the oven to 220°C. Line a baking tray with baking paper.
2. Sift the flour into a bowl. Add the salt, cream and lemonade and stir with a knife until mixed.
3. Gently turn out onto a lightly floured bench and pat out to 2.5cm thick (don't roll or knead). Using a 6cm scone cutter or a glass, cut out scones and place onto the prepared baking tray.
4. Whisk the egg and milk together and brush over the top of each scone. Bake for 10–12 minutes, until risen and golden brown. Cool on a wire rack.

COSMOPOLITAN

MARCH 2014

Supermodel
**ROBYN
LAWLEY**
*Ending the
"thigh gap"
obsession*

★ FASHION REPLAY ★

50+

ways to wear
your wardrobe
differently

Is your ex trying to
out-happy you?

DIY kink

Role play
for rookies

Plus! **The right way
to make a sex tape**

**PERFECT
FALSE
LASHES**
in 30 seconds!

go for it!

Everything you need to know to
**START YOUR
OWN BUSINESS**

SHE HAD
UNSAFE
SEX ONCE
...and
you won't
believe
what
happened
next

J'adore France

Oh France, could you get any more perfect? Your green rolling hills, Nutella jar-lined windows, bread so soft I cry to leave it behind, have me hooked. France taught me that extravagance has a certain simplicity to it, and that is how I tackle all my French recipes. You will see truffle heavily involved here; by far the best thing on this planet, it always adds that lush and extravagant feel, and luckily a little bit goes a long way. The gratin and quiche Lorraine immediately take me back to watching my French 'brother', Sylvain, in the kitchen, and whenever I want my veggie fix the ratatouille is hands-down a must to make.

Croque monsieur

This delectable ham and cheese number is quite the showstopper, demonstrating once again that the French craft some simple but extravagant dishes.

PREPARATION TIME: 20–25 MINUTES
COOKING TIME: 10 MINUTES
SERVES: 4

8 slices fresh French or Italian bread
1 tbsp unsalted butter
1 tbsp wholegrain mustard
4 thick-cut slices of ham
1^1/$_4$ cups grated gruyère

Cheese sauce:

2 tbsp unsalted butter
2 tbsp plain flour
1^1/$_2$ cups milk
^{1}/$_3$ cup grated parmesan
^{1}/$_4$ cup grated gruyère

1. Preheat the oven to 180°C.
2. To make the cheese sauce (also known as béchamel sauce), melt the butter in a saucepan over medium heat, then add the flour, using a fork to mix until smooth. Slowly add the milk and keep whisking with the fork until the sauce is smooth and becomes thicker. When it becomes thick and has started to bubble, remove the saucepan from the heat. Stir in the parmesan and gruyère, and set aside.
3. Place the bread slices onto a baking tray and lightly toast in the oven. Spread a little butter and wholegrain mustard onto each slice. Place a slice of ham and 2 tablespoons of gruyère each onto 4 of the bread slices.
4. Top with the remaining bread slices, followed by a large spoonful of the cheese sauce as well as a spoonful of gruyère. Bake in the oven for 6 minutes and then grill for 3–4 minutes, until the cheese has melted.

NOTE: Get an uncut loaf so you can slice the loaf yourself, and make the slices nice and thick.

Baguette ideas

A baguette is, in my opinion, a simple but brilliant way to eat a sandwich. Make sure the baguette is very fresh and buttered well. I've given you some suggestions for fillings but, really, the possibilities are endless.

Ham and swiss cheese, with wholegrain mustard.

Salami, chili flakes, tomato and mozzarella.

Vegetarian: rocket, brie and white grapes (my favourite).

Tuna baguette: Mix 2 small cans of tuna with 1 tbsp mayonnaise, 1 chopped spring onion, salt, pepper and a touch of mustard powder. Serve with salad mix on baguette.

Pancetta: Cook pancetta until crispy, and place onto baguette with sliced gruyère, baby spinach and cherry tomatoes.

Caesar baguette: grilled chicken, cos lettuce, shaved parmesan, boiled egg, cooked bacon rashers and Caesar sauce.

French toast

A delicious and loving breakfast to serve to guests.

PREPARATION TIME: 10 MINUTES
COOKING TIME: 10 MINUTES (2–3 MINUTES PER SLICE)
SERVES: 5

5 eggs
1 tbsp milk
3 tbsp cream (If you don't have any cream, milk will do the job)
5 thick slices of brioche (white bread also works as a substitute)
1 tbsp salted butter
$1/2$ cup sugar
1 tsp cinnamon

1. Whisk the eggs with a fork until blended. Add the milk and cream and using a whisk, mix until a nice pale yellow colour forms. Depending on your bread you can make the mixture thicker by adding eggs or runnier by adding milk. Don't be afraid to experiment with the consistency.
2. Transfer the mixture to a shallow dish and soak both sides of the bread.
3. Heat a frying pan and melt a little bit of the butter. Working in batches (depending on the size of your pan), cook the bread for 1–2 minutes each side, until golden brown.
4. Place the sugar and cinnamon on a plate and once the French toast is done, immediately lay it on the plate, and flip the bread over a few times until it is well and truly covered in sugar.
5. Serve immediately either on its own, or with ice-cream, bananas, Nutella, maple syrup, or any sweet topping of your preference.

French onion soup

The French created this aromatic dish because the ingredients can usually be found in the pantry.

Traditionally they would put the soup on in the morning and let it simmer all day; however, this recipe cuts down the time immensely. It's a crowd-pleaser.

PREPARATION TIME: 25 MINUTES
COOKING TIME: 30–40 MINUTES
SERVES: 4–5

6 brown onions, peeled and sliced thinly
4 tbsp salted butter
2 tbsp olive oil
4 cups good-quality beef stock
1 cup chicken stock
3 sprigs fresh thyme, plus fresh leaves to serve
1 day-old baguette, sliced
600g gruyére, sliced
1 tbsp grated parmesan

1. In a large saucepan or heavy-based casserole, sauté the onion in the butter and olive oil for about 5–10 minutes, until transparent, but not brown.
2. Add the stock and thyme, and season with salt and freshly ground black pepper. I tend to use to 3 teaspoons of salt, but it depends on your personal taste. Bring to a simmer and cook, covered, on low heat for 30–40 minutes.
3. Place the soup into a ovenproof bowl (or keep in the casserole dish), and put the bread on top. Slice the gruyére and lay it on the bread to cover it. Top with parmesan, and place under a hot grill to cook the top.
4. Once the cheese is melted and slightly bubbly, remove from the grill and sprinkle with thyme leaves.
5. You can make this soup ahead of time, but prepare the cheesy bread just before serving.

NOTE: It's much easier to slice the onion with a mandolin slicer, but this has a very sharp blade, so be careful of your hands. When slicing the onions, I wear goggles and a snorkel to help combat the onion sting!

Potato gratin

My French 'brother' Florent gave me this recipe. In France they do many variations of the gratin, using cauliflower and other seasonal vegetables from their garden. For extra flavour, you might like to add bacon to the recipe.

   This recipe will work for most vegetables (if you don't want to use potatoes), but the cooking time will differ.

COOKING TIME: 1 HOUR
PREPARATION TIME: 20 MINUTES
SERVES: 6

1kg potatoes
4 cups cream
2 garlic cloves, crushed
2$\frac{1}{4}$ cups grated gruyère

1. Preheat the oven to 180°C.
2. Peel the potatoes and cut into thin slices. Pour some of the cream onto the bottom of a 30 x 23cm ovenproof dish.
3. Layer the ingredients into the dish, keeping some of the gruyère for the top, and season with salt and pepper throughout.
4. Top with the remaining gruyère. Bake for at least one hour, until potatoes are tender and the top is golden brown and bubbling.

Quiche Lorraine

When I lived in France on exchange my other French 'brother', Sylvain, would make this delicious quiche Lorraine. He would usually buy the pastry pre-made at the local supermarket. I've written an easy quiche crust recipe below to save you the trip.

    The French always make their quiches with crème fraîche, which you may or may not be able to find. You can substitute cream in the filling and sour cream in the pastry if you like.

PREPARATION TIME: 45 MINUTES
COOKING TIME: 1 HOUR
SERVES: 6–8

Crust:

2 cups plain flour
150g salted butter, cubed
1 egg
2 tsp crème fraîche (or sour cream)

Filling:

3 bacon rashers, chopped
1$^1/_2$ cups crème fraîche (or cream)
5 eggs
$^1/_4$ tsp each pepper and paprika
150g gruyère (or vintage cheddar), grated
120g diced ham

1. To make the crust, sift the flour into a bowl. Add the butter and use your fingertips to rub it into the flour until it resembles fine breadcrumbs. Create a well in the centre of the flour and break the egg into it. Slowly mix with a fork.

2. After the egg is combined, add the crème fraîche, making sure to keep mixing until it forms a dough. Knead the dough for 1 minute then wrap in cling wrap and refrigerate for 30 minutes (chilling prevents pastry shrinkage).

3. Preheat the oven to 170°C and grease a 28cm loose-bottomed tart tin. Allow the dough to soften a little then roll it out and line the prepared tin. Cover the pastry with a sheet of baking paper and fill with pie weights or uncooked rice. Bake for 15 minutes, then remove the paper and weights and cook a further 8–10 minutes, until the pastry is dry and lightly golden. Set aside to cool.

4. For the filling, preheat the oven to 180°C. Cook the bacon in a frying pan until lightly browned.

5. Combine the crème fraîche, eggs, pepper, paprika and 3 tablespoons of the gruyère. Pour into the pastry shell, then add the diced ham and bacon.

6. Sprinkle the remaining gruyère evenly over the top and bake for 35 minutes, or until set and golden brown. This can be made a day ahead and reheated.

Truffle fries

In New York we often eat truffle fries with grated parmesan, served on a skillet.

PREPARATION TIME: 20 MINUTES + 1 HOUR SOAKING
COOKING TIME: 15–20 MINUTES
SERVES: 4

4 large potatoes, peeled
vegetable oil, for frying
$^3/_4$ tsp truffle salt (add more or less as desired)

1. Cut the potatoes into thin chips. Place into a bowl of ice-cold water for an hour. Drain and pat dry with paper towel when ready to cook.
2. Half fill a large saucepan (or deep-fryer) with oil. Heat until around 175°C (or when the chips bubble when placed in the oil).
3. Fry the chips in batches for 3 minutes each batch, until partially cooked. Don't overcrowd the pan or the temperature will drop too much. Transfer each batch onto paper towels to drain.
4. Increase the heat to high (200°C). Re-fry the chips in batches for 1–2 minutes, depending on the chip size, or until golden and crisp. Frying twice gives an extra crispy finish.
5. Sprinkle with the truffle salt and serve immediately.

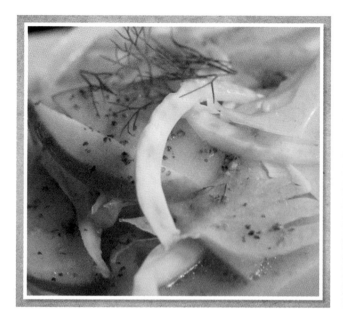

2 fennel bulbs, very thinly sliced
   (keep some fronds)
2 green apples, quartered,
   cored and finely sliced

Dressing:
$1/4$ cup extra virgin olive oil
$1/2$ cup white wine vinegar
2 tsp lemon juice
$1 1/2$ tbsp wholegrain or Dijon
   mustard
1 tsp mayonnaise
drizzle of honey

Apple fennel salad

PREPARATION TIME: 15 MINUTES
SERVES: 4

1. To make the dressing, combine the ingredients in a screwtop jar, seal tightly and shake to combine. Season to taste with salt and freshly ground black pepper.
2. Combine the fennel and apples together. Just before serving, add the dressing and gently toss through. Garnish with reserved fennel fronds.

NOTE: The fennel can be prepared ahead of time. Keep covered in the fridge. Cut the apples close to serving time or they will go brown. You can prevent the browning process by sprinkling lemon juice over the apples.

Truffle mash

I first heard about truffles while I was living in France. Vendors would sell them at weekend markets after striking gold by finding them in their backyards. They are quite odd, but so delicious. The smell of truffles cooking is by far my favourite aroma.

PREPARATION TIME: 10 MINUTES
COOKING TIME: ABOUT 10 MINUTES
SERVES: 2–4

4 potatoes (1kg)
1 tbsp salted butter
1-2 tbsp cream
truffle salt
1 tsp truffle oil

1. Peel the potatoes, chop into large chunks and cook in a saucepan of boiling water until soft.
2. Drain well, then add the butter. Cover and stand for 1 minute.
3. Once the butter has semi-melted, add the cream and mash the potatoes until smooth.
4. Add truffle salt and oil to your taste.

Roasted veggie fondue

I cooked this on one of my first dates with my current partner. Wanting to impress him, I decided an old classic fondue would be good for two. Problem was I didn't have a fondue set. Luckily, this recipe is easy and stress-free – all you need is a roasting dish, brie and your chosen vegetables, and suddenly you have your very own fondue. I tend to use root vegetables as I think they roast better and go with the melted brie amazingly, but you can use any vegetables you want.

PREPARATION TIME: 20 MINUTES
COOKING TIME: ABOUT 35–40 MINUTES
SERVES: 2

1 green capsicum, roughly chopped
8 small potatoes, halved
8 small Brussels sprouts, left whole
1 red capsicum, roughly chopped
1 yellow capsicum, roughly chopped
1 red onion, roughly chopped
$^1/_2$ sweet potato, roughly chopped
5 mushrooms (I like portobello or button)
2 tbsp extra virgin olive oil
3 sprigs fresh rosemary, pulled apart
3 tsp Herbes de Provence, to sprinkle
1 whole wheel (250g) of good-quality double brie

1. Preheat the oven to 200°C and line a large baking tray with baking paper. Arrange vegetables onto tray (excluding mushrooms), drizzle with olive oil and season with rosemary, herbs, salt and pepper. Roast for 30 minutes, turning the vegetables occasionally, then add the mushrooms and cook for another 10 minutes.

2. Use a knife to carve some scratches on top of the brie, then place it in the centre of the tray (so as it cooks it opens up). Cook for a further 5–10 minutes.

3. Voila! You have fondue. Serve with skewers for dipping the vegies if you have them, otherwise forks work fine.

NOTE: Herbes de Provence is my favourite mix of herbs. Originating from Provence, France, right near where I lived, usually it consists of rosemary, thyme, oregano and marjoram. This dish is great to share at dinner parties – just increase the quantities as needed.

Ratatouille

I had an amazing lunch cooked for me by a friend in the south of France, where this dish originated. She added chicken and potatoes to the ratatouille and it was divine. This dish is truly a crowd-pleaser.

PREPARATION TIME: 30 MINUTES
COOKING TIME: 2 HOURS
SERVES: 8–10

2 large eggplant, cut into bite-sized cubes
1 tbsp salt, plus extra for cooking
2 tbsp olive oil
2 brown onions, chopped
3 different coloured capsicum, chopped
6–8 medium zucchini, chopped
3–4 garlic cloves, crushed
4 large tomatoes, chopped
2 bay leaves
4–5 thyme sprigs
$1/4$ cup roughly chopped loosely packed basil, plus extra for garnish

1. Place the eggplant into a strainer set over a bowl and toss with the salt. Set aside.
2. Heat 2 tsp of the oil in a large (6-litre capacity) flameproof casserole dish over medium-high heat. Add the onion and a generous pinch of salt. Sauté until the onion has softened and is just beginning to brown. Add capsicum and continue cooking for 5 minutes. Transfer the onion and capsicum to a large bowl.
3. Add another 1 tsp of oil to the pot and sauté the zucchini with a generous pinch of salt for about 5 minutes or until soft and starting to brown. Transfer the zucchini to the bowl with the onion and capsicum.
4. Rinse and drain the eggplant then, using your hands, squeeze gently to remove excess moisture. Heat 3 tsp of olive oil and sauté the eggplant until it looks slightly transparent. Add the eggplant to the bowl with the other vegetables.
5. Heat remaining oil and lightly cook the garlic before adding the tomatoes, bay leaves and thyme sprigs. Scrape the bottom of the pan as you stir in the tomatoes to loosen the brown build-up from cooking. Return all the vegetables to the pot and stir until everything is mixed.
6. Bring to a simmer, then reduce heat to low. Cook for $1^1/2$ hours, stirring every 30 minutes, for a rich silky stew. If you prefer the vegetables slightly firmer cook for only 30 minutes.
7. Remove the bay leaves and thyme sprigs. Just before taking the ratatouille off the heat, stir in the basil. and season with salt and pepper to taste

NOTE: Ratatouille often tastes better the next day. I love incorporating it into an omelette the following morning, just by mixing 4 eggs with a dash of milk and $3/4$ cup of ratatouille.

Basic crepes

My friends and I would often throw crepe parties when I lived in France. We'd use a large crepe pan that would cook 6 crepes at a time. We placed the crepe pan in the middle of the table with all the condiments around and everyone would make their own.

They are so simple, yet so amazing. I remember finding this one creperie tucked away from the busy streets of Paris, where they created the best Nutella and banana crepe of my life. Good news is, you won't need to book a flight to Paris to get a great crepe. You can use this recipe to serve them anytime to your family and friends with your choice of toppings. The key to keep in mind is that crepes should be thin. I suggest using a wooden T-shaped crepe spreader.

PREPARATION TIME: 10 MINUTES
COOKING TIME: DEPENDENT ON PAN BUT
USUALLY ABOUT 1 MINUTE PER CREPE
SERVES: 6–8

2 eggs
1 cup plain flour
$1/2$ cup milk
$1/2$ cup water
for sweet crepes, add 1 teaspoon sugar
for savory crepes, add $1/4$ teaspoon of salt

1. Combine all ingredients using an electric mixer for about 1–2 minutes, until smooth. I usually pour the mixture through a sieve to remove any lumps.
2. Grease either a crepe maker or a non-stick frying pan.
3. Dollop a spoonful of batter into the centre and spread evenly and quickly (remembering a crepe is thin). They cook very fast so you'll need do this as fast as possible. Use a T-shaped crepe spreader to make this process easier.
4. Top with your choice of toppings. Fold in half and then fold again.
5. Serve immediately.

Apple tart

My French family would make this very easy dessert most nights. In France they have an amazing dough that comes pre-made, so all you need to do is roll it out, add the ingredients and bake! I love this recipe because I add a secret apple compote that gives it a stronger apple flavour.

PREPARATION TIME: 30 MINUTES
COOKING TIME: 30–40 MINUTES
SERVES: 6

1 quantity Classic Sweet Pastry (page 45) or Non-Shrink Pastry (page 44), cooked and cooled

Filling:

7–8 apples (use golden delicious if you can get them)
juice of 1 lemon, plus extra for the slices
1 tbsp sugar
30g salted butter, cut into small cubes
1 tbsp apricot jam + 2 tsp extra butter for the glaze

1. Preheat the oven to 175°C.
2. Peel half the apples, leaving just a little skin on, and cut into small cubes. Put the apple cubes into a saucepan and add the lemon juice. (This helps keep the apple a nice light colour and adds a little tart flavour.) Stir in the sugar and 2 teaspoons of water. Cook, covered, on low heat for about 20 minutes. You'll know they're ready when the pieces can easily be broken apart with a spoon, but not like mush, more like apple sauce.
3. While the apples are cooking, peel the rest of the apples, and slice them as thinly as possible. Toss with a little lemon juice to prevent browning. When the stewed apples are ready, remove from heat and spread over the base of the tart shell.
4. Arrange the slices of apple on top in a spiral to conceal the stewed apple below. Make sure you add plenty of slices as the apples will shrink while they cook. Dot the cubed butter over the top. Bake for 35 minutes at 175°C.
5. For the glaze, put the apricot jam and extra butter in a small saucepan and heat until melted and combined. Glaze the entire apple tart using a pastry brush. This is delicious with homemade (or good-quality purchased) vanilla ice-cream or custard.

ELLE

www.elle.fr

Sandales derbys baskets
TOUTES NOS ENVIES À TOUS LES PRIX

NOUVEAU PRIX **2€**

CHEVEUX
ON VEUT TOUTES UN CARRÉ

BONS PLANS VACANCES
DES PETITS COINS DE PARADIS PRÈS DE CHEZ VOUS

tendance
UN POTAGER SUR MON BALCON

MODE RONDE ET FASHION
le bon shopping et les bons mix

SOLIDAIRE
UN SALON DE BEAUTÉ POUR RETROUVER L'ESTIME DE SOI

ANTICANCER
10 RECETTES FACILES ET SAVOUREUSES

Après "Indignez-vous !"...
MARREZ-VOUS !
NOTRE NOUVEAU COMBAT

vite fait, bien fait
LA MERINGUE ON ADORE

M 01648 - 3406 - F: 2,00 €

HEBDOMADAIRE. 8 AVRIL 2011

FRANCE MÉTROPOLITAINE 2 € . DOM avion 4,70 € . BEL 2,30 € . CH 4,70 FS. A 4 € . AND 2 € . CDN $ 5.25. D 4 € . ESP 3,30 € . FIN 5,50 € . GR 4,20 € . IRL 4,40 € . ITA 3,30 € . LUX 2,30 € . MAR 30 DH . NC 1 200 F. CFP. NL 4,10 € . POLY FR 1 000 F. CFP. PORT cont 3,30 € . TUN 4 DT. USA $ 5.25.

American Journey

I think America often gets a bad reputation from its many fast food restaurants and mass-produced GMO food products. In all honesty some of my favourite dishes exist only in America. Every state has something different. New Orleans is known for its po'boys, Philadelphia has its cheese steaks, and New York pizza is absolutely the best. It was in New York that I fulfilled my childhood dream of eating out almost daily.

I prefer staying in these days, but I still enjoy making what those restaurants had to offer in the comfort of my own home. Whether it is a slow-roasted turkey dinner, pulled pork or the famous chicken biscuit, this is a chapter worth exploring.

Baked avocado with egg

A glamorous way to serve up eggs on a cold winter's day.

PREPARATION TIME: 2 MINUTES
COOKING TIME: 15–20 MINUTES
SERVES: 2

2 large avocados
4 eggs
olive oil, to drizzle
cooked bacon bits to sprinkle on top, optional
good quality bread (I suggest sourdough but use your preference), toasted and
  buttered

1. Preheat the oven to 200°C. Halve and deseed the avocado and remove enough of the flesh to leave space for an egg.
2. Scrunch and fold foil and place on a baking tray, to hold the avocado halves while they cook.
3. Crack an egg into the centre of each avocado half. Season with salt and pepper, and bake for 15–20 minutes or until the egg is cooked.
4. Drizzle olive oil on top and add more salt and pepper, to taste. Serve with buttered toast. Serve sprinkled with bacon bits, if using, with buttered toast on the side.

Steak and eggs

I made this dish one morning for my partner and myself. It actually originated in Australia but was passed through to America during the Pacific War. I now see it on most diner menus in New York and I think that's where I got the idea from.

PREPARATION TIME: 10 MINUTES
COOKING TIME: 10 MINUTES
SERVES: 1

¼ tsp steak seasoning
1 filet mignon steak (5cm thick)
½ tsp salted butter
2 eggs

Optional:

2 slices baguette
2 slices swiss cheese
½ avocado
5 cherry tomatoes

1. Rub the seasoning into the steak. Melt half the butter in a frying pan and seal both sides of the steak.
2. Add 2 tablespoons of water to the pan and place a lid over the steak. Cook for 3–4 minutes on low heat for medium-rare, or to your liking.
3. Drain the water and add the remaining butter to the pan. Reseal both sides of the steak. In a separate pan, fry the eggs to your liking (in a little butter or oil if not using a non-stick pan).

NOTE: If you like, serve the steak as a sandwich on toasted baguette, with melted swiss cheese, sliced avocado and cherry tomatoes. This goes well with Dijon mustard or barbecue sauce.

Breakfast burritos

If I had to choose one last meal, this might be it. I had my first breakfast burrito in New Orleans at a music festival, where we camped in these really cool tents (it was more like glamping). One morning we were served a delicious burrito. These are popular in America, and I must admit I'd never really wanted to try one, but I assure you this is an experience that should not be missed.

PREPARATION TIME: 15–20 MINUTES
COOKING TIME: 35 MINUTES
SERVES: 4

1 cup rice
4 thick-cut bacon rashers, chopped
2 spicy Italian sausages
2 potatoes, cut into chunks
1 yellow or red capsicum, cut into strips
2 tsp olive oil
1 cup grated cheddar
4 tortillas
5 eggs
1 tbsp cream
$^3/_4$ cup canned black beans, rinsed, drained and heated
sour cream, hot sauce and tomato salsa to serve

1. Cook the rice in a saucepan of boiling water for 10 minutes, or until tender. Drain and set aside.
2. Fry the bacon until crispy, followed by the sausage. Remove from the pan and set aside, leaving the remaining fat in the pan. Chop the bacon and cut the sausages lengthwise once they have cooled slightly.
3. Steam the potatoes for about 5 minutes or until slightly soft, then fry them in the bacon fat until crisp. Season with salt and freshly ground black pepper.
4. In a separate frying pan, sauté the capsicum in the olive oil until soft. Set aside.
5. Sprinkle some cheddar onto each tortilla and gently heat in the oven or microwave until the cheese has just melted.
6. Whisk the eggs together with cream and cook gently in the frying pan, to make scrambled eggs.
7. Layer the tortillas with the cooked ingredients and beans. Top with a tablespoon of sour cream, as well as a dash of hot sauce and some tomato salsa. Serve immediately.

Notes

Breakfast pie

PREPARATION TIME: 15 MINUTES
COOKING TIME: 20 MINUTES
SERVES: 4

4 thick-cut bacon rashers, chopped
1 Italian sausage, cut into small chunks (spicy optional)
6 eggs
1 tbsp cream
1 tbsp finely grated parmesan
1 sheet frozen puff pastry, thawed
1 egg white, lightly beaten
4 small chunks brie
2 tbsp vintage cheddar

1. Preheat the oven to 200°C and line four 12cm springform tins with baking paper.
2. Fry the bacon and sausage until the bacon is nearly crispy. Cool slightly then roughly chop the bacon. Whisk the eggs and cream together with a fork and stir in the parmesan.
3. Cut the puff pastry into 4 squares and brush with egg white. Place the puff pastry into the tin, brushed side up. Lay the bacon down first, then pour in the egg mixture. Add the sausage and brie, then sprinkle with the cheddar.
4. Bake for 15 minutes, until the filling has risen and set and the top is golden.

Buffalo wings

I had my first traditional buffalo wings at the gridiron grand final last year. Super Bowl is a huge deal in America – it literally stops the nation.

These little numbers are so delicious and are always served with ranch or blue cheese dressing, carrots and celery.

I prefer to bake mine rather than deep-fry them, as they taste the same without the extra fuss or mess.

If you are cooking for a large group, this recipe can be easily doubled.

PREPARATION TIME: 35–40 MINUTES
COOKING TIME: 40 MINUTES
SERVES: 3–4

1kg chicken wings
1/4 tsp salt
3 tbsp olive oil
2 tsp paprika
1/4 cup plain flour
3 tbsp butter
1 tbsp hot sauce (Cholula brand if you can get it – it's the best one)
1 tbsp white vinegar
2 tsp Worcestershire sauce
1 tsp Tabasco, or more to taste, depending on how spicy you like them

1. Preheat the oven to 180°C and line a large baking tray with baking paper.
2. In a bowl, coat the chicken wings with the salt, 2 tablespoons of the olive oil and 1 teaspoon of the paprika. Add the flour and toss to coat the wings.
3. Place the wings evenly apart on the tray and drizzle with the remaining olive oil. Bake for 20 minutes.
4. Turn the wings and bake for another 20 minutes. Always check one wing before you take them out to make sure they are fully cooked, as the time needed will depend on the size of the wings.
5. To make the sauce for the wings, melt the butter in a saucepan and add the hot sauce, vinegar, Worcestershire sauce, Tabasco and remaining paprika. Bring to the boil, then simmer for 3 minutes.
6. Coat the wings in the sauce when you are ready to serve. Serve with ranch or blue cheese dressing (see my recipe on the next page for a good home-made dressing).

Ranch dressing

I'm not a fan of store-bought sauces, so I make my own dressing with the following ingredients:

$1/2$ cup mayonnaise
1 tbsp sour cream
1 tsp garlic powder
1 tsp onion powder
1 tsp salt
1 tsp chopped parsley, dried or fresh
1 tsp dried dill
1 tsp dried coriander

Combine all ingredients and chill for 30 minutes prior to serving.

Chicken biscuit

This little southern dish packs a punch. Don't get confused by the name; the biscuit is actually a version of a buttery scone. I didn't discover this recipe until I moved to America. My friend took me down the road to a little restaurant called Pies 'n' Thighs in Brooklyn. I am still thanking her to this day for taking me there. Good news is you can make it just as well at home.

PREPARATION TIME: 1 HOUR
COOKING TIME: 45 MINUTES
SERVES: 4

Biscuit (buttery scone):

2 cups plain flour (plus 1 tbsp extra, for dusting)
1 tbsp baking powder
2 tsp white sugar
$^1/_4$ tsp salt
$^1/_3$ cup cold salted butter, cubed
1 cup buttermilk
butter, to serve

Fried chicken:

vegetable oil, to deep-fry
4 eggs
1 cup self-raising flour
$^1/_2$ cup fine breadcrumbs
1 tsp ground black pepper
1 tsp salt
1 tsp mustard powder
1 tsp garlic powder
2 large chicken breasts, cut into thick pieces (you can use any cut of chicken for this)
1 cup hot red pepper sauce or buffalo sauce and honey, to serve

1. To make the biscuits, line a baking tray with baking paper. Combine the dry ingredients in a bowl or a food processor. Rub in the butter with your fingertips, or process until the mixture is the consistency of breadcrumbs. Add the buttermilk, and mix until just combined – do not over-mix.

2. Turn the dough out onto a lightly floured work bench, and pat out to 2.5cm thick. Don't knead the dough, just handle it very gently – it will be a little sticky.

3. Using a floured glass or cookie cutter about 9cm in diameter, cut out biscuits and place onto the baking tray. Refrigerate for 30 minutes. (You can use this time to prepare the chicken.) Preheat the oven to 220°C.

4. Bake the biscuits for 15–20 minutes, until slightly brown on the edges.

5. For the fried chicken, half fill a large saucepan (or deep-fryer) with oil, and heat over medium-high heat (it should be 180°C – use a deep frying thermometer to test).

6. Whisk the eggs and $1/3$ cup water together in a large bowl. Combine the flour, breadcrumbs and spices on a large plate. Working in batches to avoid overcrowding the pan, dip the chicken into the egg, then place onto the flour plate. Rotate the chicken so it is covered in the flour mixture.

7. Pop it straight into the hot oil. Cook for 10–15 minutes, making sure to turn the chicken every few minutes. (I recommend at 8 minutes cutting a piece in the middle to see if it's cooked. Overcooking will dry the chicken out.)

8. When cooked through, fill a bowl with hot sauce. Coat the fried chicken in the sauce.

9. Serve immediately, with a buttered biscuit and a squeeze of honey.

Slow-roasted jerk chicken

This chicken recipe produces outstanding results. The brine and Jamaican-inspired dry rub combined yield a juicy meat with crisp flavourful skin. A great way to spice up a Sunday roast.

PREPARATION TIME: 30 MINUTES + 6–9 HOURS BRINING
COOKING TIME: 2 HOURS
SERVES: 4–6

2.2kg large chicken – halve dry rub ingredients if chicken weighs 1–1.5kg
2 onions (brown or red), finely sliced
5 thyme sprigs
2 garlic cloves, chopped
$\frac{1}{2}$ lemon
1–2 cups chicken stock

Brine:

2L cold water
$\frac{1}{2}$ cup salt
$\frac{1}{2}$ cup brown sugar
$\frac{1}{2}$ cup white vinegar
$\frac{1}{2}$ cup chicken stock
juice of 1 lemon
1 garlic clove, crushed

Dry rub:

4 tbsp brown sugar
$1\frac{1}{2}$ tbsp paprika
1 tbsp sea salt flakes
3 tbsp chili powder (change to 1–2 tsp if you don't like spicy)
1 tsp dried chilli flakes
1 tsp garlic powder
3 tsp ground black pepper
$\frac{1}{2}$ tsp ground cumin
$\frac{1}{2}$ tsp finely grated lemon zest

1. Combine all the brine ingredients in a large bowl (big enough for the chicken to be submerged). Add the chicken, cover and refrigerate for 6–9 hours.

2. When ready to roast, preheat the oven to 150°C. Spread onions evenly into a roasting pan and place a wire rack on top. Drain the chicken from the brine and pat dry inside and out with paper towels. Place onto the rack and place thyme, garlic and lemon inside the chicken.

3. Combine the dry rub ingredients and rub all over the chicken (don't worry if some of the mixture falls into the pan, leave it there). Carefully pour chicken stock into the roasting pan, without letting it touch the chicken. Cover the chicken breast with foil.

4. Roast for 1 1/2 hours, then take off the foil and cook for a further 30 minutes. Increase the temperature to 220°C for the last 10 minutes of cooking, to make the skin crisp.

5. Check to make sure your chicken is cooked by piercing a thigh to see if the juices run clear, or by using a digital thermometer (the safest way) which should reach 74°C. Take out of the oven, cover loosely with foil and let sit for 10 minutes before carving and serving.

   NOTE: This is best served with rice. It's great to shred the remaining chicken you don't eat for a cheesy quesadilla the next day. The drippings are very salty, and do not make a good gravy.

In America this cut is known as 'Boston Butt'.

Pulled pork

This recipe really creates juicy, tender pulled pork. It's an excellent and different dish to bring to a barbecue served with bread rolls, barbecue sauce and coleslaw.

   This recipe makes a large amount, but it freezes well and can be used in various other dishes.

PREPARATION TIME: 20 MINUTES
COOKING TIME: 7-8 HOURS
SERVES: 8+

3 brown onions
5 medium garlic cloves
350ml chicken stock
1 tbsp brown sugar
3 tbsp chilli powder
3 tbsp sea salt
$1/2$ tsp ground cumin
$1/2$ fennel seeds
$1/2$ tsp ground cinnamon
4–6kg bone-in pork shoulder, any twine removed
1 bay leaf
1–2 cups of your favourite barbecue sauce

1. Preheat the oven to 110°C.
2. Finely slice the onions and garlic and lay evenly in a heavy-based flameproof casserole dish. Slowly pour in the chicken stock.
3. In a small bowl, combine the sugar, chilli powder, salt, cumin, fennel and cinnamon.
4. Pat the pork dry with paper towels. Rub the spice mixture entirely over the pork shoulder, and scatter any leftover spice mixture inside the pot.
5. Carefully place the pork into the casserole dish, on top of the liquid and onions. Add the bay leaf, then cover and place into the oven.
6. After about 7–8 hours, check the pork. Once it starts pulling away from the bone and shreds easily, it's ready. Strain the pork but keep $1/4$ cup of the liquid. Cover the pork with foil and sit for 15 minutes.
7. Transfer the pork to a large bowl (or return it to the pot) and, using two forks, shred the meat, removing any large lumps of fat.
8. Moisten the meat with the reserved liquid and 1 cup barbecue sauce, adding more to your taste. Stir until it is mixed through.

Cobb salad

A staple dish in many American diners, this one ranks highly on my list of favourite salads. Sure, it's delicious, but I also love the arrangement of it on the plate. Rather than being tossed together, it is composed in a particular way.

PREPARATION TIME: 30 MINUTES
SERVES: 4–5

1 iceberg lettuce, cored and shredded
1 cos lettuce, chopped
125g blue cheese, crumbled
6 bacon rashers, cooked and roughly chopped
3 hard-boiled eggs, peeled and cut into small cubes
2 medium tomatoes, cut into small cubes
1 avocado, peeled, pitted, and cut into 1cm cubes
1 chicken breast fillet, cooked and cut into 1cm cubes
1 tbsp chopped chives

Dressing:
$^3/_4$ tsp mustard powder
1 tsp Worcestershire sauce
$^1/_4$ teaspoon sugar
$^1/_2$ cup canola oil
$^1/_2$ cup extra-virgin olive oil
$^1/_4$ cup red wine vinegar
1 tbsp lemon juice
1 garlic clove, crushed
1 tbsp mayonnaise

1. Combine the lettuces in a large bowl or on a platter. Next, in neat rows, place the blue cheese, bacon, eggs, tomatoes, avocado and chicken alongside each other.
2. To make the dressing, combine all ingredients in a blender and blend for 1 minute. If you do not have a blender, mix together in a jar. Season with salt and pepper to taste. If making the dressing ahead of time, refrigerate in an airtight container.
3. Drizzle the dressing over if you are about to serve, or keep the dressing on the side until ready to serve.
4. Top with the chives.

NOTE: Leave out the bacon and chicken for a vegetarian alternative.

2 avocados
1/2 tsp lemon juice
1/4 garlic clove, finely chopped
1/4 jalapeño chilli, finely
    chopped (add more if you
    want more spice!)
1 large tomato, roughly
    chopped
2 tsp finely chopped red onion
2 tsp chopped fresh coriander

Guacamole

In our family this is cherished above everything else. Whenever my mum or I would make guacamole we had a habit of keeping the news secret. But as people entered the kitchen and noticed it sitting there, it became the Battle of the Guac! This is my trademark recipe and I just love it!

PREPARATION TIME: 10 MINUTES
SERVES: 2–4

Mash the avocado in a bowl and add the lemon juice. Mix in the garlic and chilli, then the remaining ingredients. Season with salt to taste, then serve fresh.

Fresh mint pasta salad

This dish is great for a barbecue, and can be made a day ahead.

PREPARATION TIME: 20 MINUTES
COOKING TIME: ABOUT 12 MINUTES
SERVES: 6 AS A SIDE DISH

3 cups penne
2 cups broad beans, skinned (fresh or frozen)
2 spring onions, diced
1 cup fresh mint leaves, ripped or chopped
$3/4$ cup crumbled feta or ricotta

Dressing:
$1/2$ cup lemon juice
$1/2$ cup good-quality mayonnaise
2 tbsp olive oil

1. Cook the pasta as directed on the package until al dente, adding the broad beans for the last 3 minutes of cooking. Drain in a colander.
2. In a big salad bowl combine the pasta, broad beans, spring onions and mint.
3. To make the dressing, whisk the ingredients together. Toss through the salad.
4. Top with the feta or ricotta and stir together.

Prawn chowder

I derived this recipe from the New England clam chowder. It's similar, but uses prawns instead. When I take road trips to the Hamptons I always have to stop at the chowder house near Montauk to get my chowder fix. It's perfect for a winter's day.

PREPARATION TIME: 20 MINUTES
COOKING TIME: 20 MINUTES
SERVES: 4

6 bacon rashers
1 large brown onion, finely chopped
2 large sebago potatoes, chopped into rough 2.5cm cubes
400ml thickened cream
3 tbsp butter
20 green prawns, peeled and deveined
2 celery stalks, finely chopped

1. Chop the bacon and cook in a large pot until it turns crispy. Add the onion and cook for another 2 minutes.
2. Add the potato and 1 1/2 cups water. Bring to the boil then reduce the heat and simmer for 10–15 minutes, until the potatoes are slightly soft and the water has evaporated. Turn off heat and add the cream and 2 tablespoons of the butter.
3. Heat the remaining butter in a frying pan, and sauté the prawns and celery until the prawns turn pink. Add to the chowder and stir through.
4. Season with salt and freshly ground black pepper. Serve immediately with either oyster crackers (an American plain cracker) or toast.

Brisket

$^1/_2$ tsp salt
$^1/_2$ tsp cracked ground pepper
1.2–3kg good quality brisket
1 tbsp extra virgin olive oil
2 onions, chopped
2 large carrots, chopped (or 4 small)
1 fennel bulb, chopped
3 celery stalks, chopped
$1^1/_2$ cups red wine
$1^1/_2$ cups beef stock
2 cups chicken stock
$^1/_2$ cup bourbon
3 sprigs thyme
3 sprigs rosemary
2 bay leaves
200g black liquorice
1 tbsp fennel seed
2 tbsp barbecue sauce
3 tsp butter
cooked soft polenta, optional, to serve

1. Preheat the oven to 115°C.
2. Combine the salt and cracked pepper and rub all over the meat. Heat the oil in a heavy-based flameproof casserole dish and brown the meat on all sides. Add the vegetables.
3. Add the wine, stock and bourbon to the pot. Make sure the brisket is fully covered by liquid, and top up with extra stock if necessary. Add the herbs, liquorice and fennel seeds.
4. Bring to the boil uncovered, then cover and transfer to the oven. Cook for 6–7 hours, and check the meat before removing. It should fall apart easily when touched. If not, cook a little longer, checking regularly. Set aside to cool for 1 hour.
5. Remove the brisket from the braising liquid and place into a bowl. Cover immediately with foil so it doesn't steam dry. Strain the braising liquid into a saucepan then add the barbecue sauce. Add the butter and bring the liquid to a simmer. Cook for about 5 minutes, until reduced, dark and glossy.
6. Tear apart the brisket, removing most but not all of the fat, then place it into the sauce. Serve on a bed of polenta if you like.

Brisket is very popular in America, but it can be a difficult meat to cook. When done right, it will melt in your mouth.

- 4 boneless chicken breasts
- 4 tbsp pesto
- 400g mozzarella
- 8 thin slices prosciutto
- 3 cups cherry tomatoes, halved
- 1/3 cup dry white wine
- 1 tbsp extra virgin olive oil

To serve with:

- 375g fettuccine
- 4 tbsp cream
- 100g finely grated parmesan

Chicken wrapped in prosciutto with pesto and fettuccine

PREPARATION TIME: 20 MINUTES
COOKING TIME: 20–25 MINUTES
SERVES: 4

1. Preheat the oven to 220°C.
2. Pat the chicken dry with paper towels. Place the chicken breasts on a chopping board and make a deep cut into the side, to create a pocket. Do not cut all the way through.
3. Place 1 tablespoon of pesto into each pocket. Cut the mozzarella into 4 pieces and tuck a piece into each pocket, then wrap each chicken breast with 2 slices of prosciutto.
4. Place the chicken into a roasting pan and scatter the cherry tomatoes over the chicken. Add the wine to the pan. Drizzle evenly with oil, and season with salt and freshly ground black pepper.
5. Roast for 20–25 minutes, making sure to test that the chicken is cooked through by piercing one breast to see if juices run clear.
6. Boil water with a touch of salt and cook fettuccine until al dente. Serve with the chicken breasts, whole or sliced up. Drizzle with cream and sprinkle with parmesan.

Homemade pesto

PREPARATION TIME: 10 MINUTES
SERVES: ENOUGH FOR A PASTA FOR 4 PEOPLE

3 cups packed fresh basil leaves
$^1/_3$ cup pine nuts
4 garlic cloves
$^3/_4$ cup extra virgin olive oil
1 cup freshly grated parmesan

1. Combine the basil and pine nuts in a food processor and pulse a few times until well chopped.
2. Add the garlic, then pulse a few more times.
3. With the motor running, slowly add the olive oil. Pause occasionally to scrape down the sides, ensuring the mixture is evenly processed.
4. Add the parmesan and pulse again until fully blended. Season with salt and freshly ground black pepper to taste.
5. Toss immediately with cooked pasta, or store in an airtight container or jar in the fridge to consume later.

8g dry yeast

1g sugar

355ml warm water

565g plain flour

18g finely ground sea salt

14g extra virgin olive oil

For the topping
(enough for 1 pizza):

2 tsp dried oregano

2 tbsp pizza sauce (I like to
combine tomato paste and
pasta sauce)

1 cup grated mozzarella

1 tbsp finely grated parmesan

extra virgin olive oil, to serve

New York pizza

Pizza and New York of course go hand in hand.

My favourite pizza place was a small, unassuming takeout joint in Brooklyn called Driggs Pizza. They had a spicy bruschetta pizza that was called 'Grandpa's slice'.

Another place that is amazing is Artichoke Pizza, and it's famous for its thick artichoke pizza topping and dough. One slice will fill you up for days.

Here is a recipe based on the classic NYC style pizza, the ones that you see in movies being folded in half to eat. The topping consists of cheese, tomato and oregano.

For a good pizza at home you will need a pizza stone (they're relatively cheap). It helps your pizza get a proper crunchy finish on the base.

The dough recipe is a quick-rise dough, courtesy of Pizza A Casa, a pizza school in East Village that helped me master pizza dough. You can use it the same day; however, in my opinion it tastes better when it's a day old.

I'd recommend using kitchen scales to get the exact measurements.

A classic NYC slice.

PREPARATION TIME: 25 MINUTES
COOKING TIME: 30 MINUTES
MAKES: DOUGH FOR 4 PIZZAS

1. Combine the yeast, sugar and water in a jug and set aside for about 15 minutes, until frothy (this activates the yeast). Combine the flour, salt and olive oil in a large bowl, and create a well in the centre.

2. Slowly pour the yeast mixture into the flour and stir until combined. Turn out onto a floured surface (marble is best) and dust your hands with flour. Knead the dough for about five minutes until is smooth. This is essential – it's what helps develop the gluten. A good way to see if the dough has been kneaded enough is to poke it. The dough should bounce back.

3. Split your dough evenly into 4 portions. Using your hands pick up one of the portions, and roll it into a seamless ball – otherwise when you roll out your dough you will have a 'fault line', which makes stretching out difficult.

4. Lightly grease 4 large bowls or containers with a touch of olive oil. Add the dough and cover with greased cling wrap. Set aside in a semi-warm place (not near the oven) for 45 minutes, to rise. If you are making a day ahead, keep in the fridge.

5. Before you start to cook, place a pizza stone inside the oven and turn the oven on the highest setting it goes (260°C and higher), without burning down the house. Heat the stone for about an hour before you want to cook the pizza.

6. Turn a dough ball out onto a floured surface, and tap it gently with your hands, down and around, so it's still a circle. Pick it up at the edge with 2 fingers and slowly turn it, allowing the pizza to stretch itself. Don't be scared if a hole appears. You can fix that later by pinching the dough together.

7. Place the dough back on the surface and, using both hands, finish stretching the pizza using what's called the DJ method – it will look like you're mixing music with the dough.

8. If your pizza is not a perfect circle, don't worry. It's going to be a lot tastier the less you fiddle with it. The more you do stretch it out the crunchier it will get, so you can adjust this depending on how you like your pizza.

9. Pick up the dough and place it onto a pizza peel (if using a pizza stone) or onto a pizza tray.

10. Mix the oregano with the sauce and spread it over the pizza, going as near to the edges as you can with the back of a spoon. Scatter the mozzarella evenly across the pizza, and top with parmesan.

11. Cook for about 8 minutes, but keep a close eye on it, as oven temperatures can vary enormously.

12. When you take it out, drizzle a little more olive oil on top and serve immediately. Repeat with remaining dough to make 3 more pizzas.

Truffle mac and cheese

Almost iconic in America, mac and cheese is a true comfort food. I've jazzed up this easy number with truffles. It's a dish to serve up to a group of hungry guests.

PREPARATION TIME: 45 MINUTES
COOKING TIME: ABOUT 25 MINUTES
SERVES: 4–5

400g macaroni
3 tbsp salted butter
3 tbsp plain flour
1 tbsp mustard powder
3 cups milk
1/2 cup finely chopped brown onion
1 bay leaf
1 tsp paprika
1 egg, lightly beaten
2 cups grated vintage cheddar
1 tsp truffle salt, plus extra to taste
1/4 cup grated parmesan
1 tbsp truffle oil
1/2 teaspoon garlic powder
real shaved truffles, optional

1. Preheat the oven to 175°C.
2. Bring a large pot of slightly salted water to boil, then cook the macaroni until it is al dente. Drain well.
3. While the pasta is cooking, melt the butter in a separate saucepan over medium-low heat. Whisk in the flour and mustard and keep stirring. Make sure there are no lumps. Stir in the milk, onion, bay leaf and paprika. Bring to a simmer and cook for ten minutes, then remove the bay leaf. Take off the heat and cool slightly.
4. Add the egg. Stir in 3/4 of the grated cheddar and season with the truffle salt. Fold through the macaroni and pour the mixture into an 8-cup capacity casserole dish.
5. Top with the remaining cheddar and the parmesan, then drizzle the truffle oil evenly over the dish.
6. Sprinkle with the garlic powder and a little extra truffle salt. (You can also sprinkle some extra paprika if desired.)
7. Bake for 15 minutes. Place under a hot grill until the cheese has turned nice and golden. Top with shaved truffles. Serve hot.

Thanksgiving

1 turkey neck
1 tbsp gravy powder
pan juices from the roast turkey

Optional:

plain flour, to thicken, though
the gravy powder will also
do the trick

Turkey gravy

PREPARATION TIME: 5 MINUTES
COOKING TIME: 35 MINUTES
MAKES: 2 CUPS

1. Place the turkey neck into a saucepan with 3½ cups of water. Bring to the boil, then reduce heat and simmer for 30 minutes. This will make the turkey stock.
2. Combine 2 cups of the turkey stock in a smaller saucepan with the gravy powder and pan juices from the roast turkey. Stir until gravy boils and thickens.
3. Serve immediately.

Turkey stuffing

I had a version of this at my very first American thanksgiving with my partner's family – it has an Italian twist. Over time I have perfected this recipe and I can guarantee it will make your guests come back for more.

I don't use this to stuff the turkey – I do that with aromatic vegetables. Stuffing can increase the cooking time of a turkey, and you risk the meat becoming dry, so I cook this in a separate dish.

PREPARATION TIME: 30 MINUTES
COOKING TIME: 35 MINUTES
SERVES: 8

1 loaf Italian bread, cut into 2.5cm cubes
2 tbsp olive oil
1kg spicy Italian sausage, skin removed (alternatively, buy mince)
8 bacon rashers, chopped
125g unsalted butter, cut into chunks
3 medium onions
4 celery stalks, chopped
5 garlic cloves, finely chopped
4 eggs, lightly beaten
1$\frac{1}{2}$ cups thickened cream
$\frac{1}{2}$ cup chicken stock or turkey stock (see page 143 for turkey stock recipe)
1$\frac{1}{2}$ cups grated parmesan
1 sprig thyme, leaves removed
$\frac{3}{4}$ cup coarsely chopped flat-leaf parsley
$\frac{1}{2}$ tsp garlic powder
$\frac{1}{2}$ cup grated vintage cheddar

1. Preheat the oven to 180°C and grease a 25 x 35cm deep baking dish with butter.
2. Spread the bread on a baking tray and toast in the oven for about 10 minutes, turning once, until dry and slightly crisp.
3. Meanwhile, heat the olive oil in a large frying pan and cook the sausage until it is nice and golden, breaking it up as you go. Place in a large bowl. Fry the bacon in the same pan until crispy, then add to the sausage.
4. Drain the oil from the pan and add the butter. Sauté the onions lightly, then add the celery and garlic. Cook for about 5 minutes, until golden. Add the vegetables and bread to the bowl.
5. Whisk together the eggs, cream, stock, 1 cup of the parmesan, the thyme and parsley. Season with salt and pepper. Stir into the mixture and refrigerate for 30 minutes.
6. Increase the oven to 220°C (while the turkey is resting). Spoon the mixture into the dish and sprinkle with the garlic powder and vintage cheddar. Cover with foil and cook for 20 minutes. Remove the foil and grill the top until golden.

Turkey roast

I've had my fair share of turkey roasts while living in the US, an unforgiving poultry that will leave many people exasperated if not cooked right. However, I've managed to make a foolproof turkey roast recipe, which should yield excellent results. By roasting with the bird facing down, you prevent the breast from drying out.

PREPARATION TIME: 30 MINUTES + 12 HOURS MARINATING
COOKING TIME: $2^{1}/_2$ HOURS + 30 MINUTES RESTING
SERVES: 8+

4–5kg organic/free range turkey (fresh will deliver better results than a frozen turkey)
2 tbsp sea salt
1 tbsp ground black pepper
2 lemons
14 garlic cloves, divided, crushed
2 bunches fresh thyme
1 bunch fresh rosemary
1 bunch fresh sage
3 onions, diced
4 bay leaves
350ml bottle apple cider
$1^{1}/_2$ cups dry white wine
4 tbsp melted butter
1 tbsp maple syrup

1. Remove the neck and giblets from the turkey and keep aside if using for gravy. Pat the turkey dry with paper towels.
2. In a small bowl, combine the salt, pepper and finely grated zest from one of the lemons. Rub the mixture all over the turkey.
3. Quarter the zested lemon, and place inside the cavity with three of the garlic cloves. Transfer the turkey to a large resealable plastic bag.
4. Wash the herbs quickly with hot water (this makes the scents stronger), and allow them to cool. Set aside one bunch of thyme for later, and place the remaining herbs, along with four of the garlic cloves, inside the bag. Seal the bag and refrigerate for at least 12 hours. You can keep it in your fridge for up to two days.
5. When you're ready to cook, remove the turkey from the fridge and take it out of the bag. Allow it to return to room temperature (about an hour). Pat dry again with paper towels.
6. Preheat the oven to 225°C. Arrange $^3/_4$ of the onions, the bay leaves and the remaining garlic into a deep roasting pan, and add the cider and wine. Place a rack into the pan.
7. Remove the lemon from inside the turkey. Quarter the remaining lemon, and place into the cavity with the reserved bunch of thyme and the remaining onion.

8. Mix together the melted butter and maple syrup, then brush over the turkey, keeping some for basting. Place the turkey breast-side down onto the rack in the roasting tray.

9. Cook for 30 minutes, then reduce the oven temperature to 175°C. Continue roasting, basting periodically with the butter and maple syrup, but not too often as the oven temperature will drop if you open the door too often.

10. After 1¼ hours, carefully turn the turkey over so it is breast-side up. Cook for a further 30–60 minutes. If you want a crispier skin, turn the heat back to 225°C. If any parts start to burn, place a small piece of foil over the burn to prevent it from burning any further.

11. Insert a digital thermometer into the thigh of the turkey, taking care not to hit the bone. Once the turkey has reached 74°C, it is safe to eat.

12. When ready, remove the turkey from the oven and cover with foil. Rest it for 30 minutes before carving. Again, this step will prevent it from drying out.

360g fresh or frozen cranberries
juice of 2 oranges
3/4 cup white sugar
1/4 tsp cornflour

Cranberry sauce

PREPARATION TIME: 10 MINUTES
COOKING TIME: 5 MINUTES
MAKES: 1 1/2 CUPS

1. Combine the cranberries, orange juice and sugar in a saucepan. Stir over low heat until sugar dissolves.
2. Mix the cornflour in a small bowl with 1 teaspoon of water until smooth. Stir into the cranberry mixture. Increase the heat and bring to the boil, then turn down the heat and simmer for 2 minutes.

Crispy fried Brussels sprouts

I used to always bake my Brussels sprouts for Thanksgiving until I was at a music festival in New York and tried crispy fried Brussels sprouts. My life was changed for the better.

The good news is, if you are making this for a Thanksgiving meal, you won't require the use of the oven, freeing up valuable oven space. (When roasting a turkey you may not have any room left.)

PREPARATION TIME: 5 MINUTES
COOKING TIME: 5 MINUTES
SERVES: 6

1. Rinse the Brussels sprouts and pat dry with a paper towel. Cut off the ends and halve. Set aside.
2. Heat the oil in a large wok or saucepan over high heat. Carefully drop small batches of the Brussels sprouts into the oil (stand back as oil can spit). Do not overcrowd the pan or the temperature will drop.
3. Cook for approximately 5 minutes, rotating a few times.
4. Place the Brussels sprouts into a bowl and season with salt and pepper. I sometimes use truffle salt for something a little more exciting. Serve immediately.

500g Brussels sprouts
4 cups sesame oil or canola oil
    (sesame is better)
truffle salt (optional)

Chocolate pie

Mary, my partner's mother, gave me this recipe, and I love it for its decadence. I've modified it over time. It's a great pie to make ahead of time.

PREPARATION TIME: 30 MINUTES
COOKING TIME: 10 MINUTES + 5 HOURS SETTING
SERVES: 8

1/2 quantity Easy Pastry Crust (page 161), cooked and cooled

Filling:

1 cup milk
1 cup thickened cream
1/2 cup caster sugar
2 tbsp cornflour
6 egg yolks, at room temperature
125g unsalted butter, chopped
170g good-quality dark chocolate, broken up (don't use cooking chocolate)
170g milk chocolate, broken up
1 tsp vanilla extract

Topping:

1/2 cup thickened cream
1 tbsp icing sugar
cocoa powder, to dust

1. To make the filling, combine the milk and cream in a saucepan and add 3 tablespoons of the sugar, stirring constantly until the sugar dissolves and the mixture simmers. Mix the cornflour and the remaining sugar in a small bowl.

2. Whisk the egg yolks in a separate bowl, then sprinkle the cornflour mixture over. Whisk for about 1 minute, until glossy.

3. Pour half the milk mixture into the yolk mixture, stirring constantly, then pour back into the saucepan with the remaining milk. Stir over low heat until thickened (do not boil). Add the butter, chocolate and vanilla, and stir until melted and smooth.

4. Pour through a sieve to remove any lumps before pouring into the pie shell. Refrigerate for 1 hour.

5. For the topping, whip the cream with icing sugar and spread on top of the chocolate filling. Dust with cocoa powder. Refrigerate for at least 5 hours before serving.

Lemon cheesecake

You can't live in New York and not eat cheesecake – and this particular recipe is so creamy and rich! It's great because if the top cracks (which is what usually happens if you're not using a huge commercial oven, or if there is a sudden drop in temperature), the extra layer you add on the end disguises it. This recipe was given to me by my partner's mother, Mary, but I've added my own Australian twist for the crust.

PREPARATION TIME: 45 MINUTES
COOKING TIME: 1 HOUR AND 10 MINUTES + 5–8 HOURS CHILLING
SERVES: 8–10

Crust:

400g Scotch Finger biscuits
2 tbsp sugar
135g salted butter, melted
(double all crust quantities if you want the crust continued on the sides, but here, I've only used the crust for the base)

Filling:

1.25kg cream cheese, at room temperature, chopped
$1^1/_2$ cups sugar
$^1/_4$ cup plain flour, sifted
$2^1/_2$ tsp finely grated lemon zest
$^1/_4$ tsp salt
1 tbsp vanilla extract
5 eggs
$^1/_2$ cup thickened cream

Topping:

$1^1/_2$ cups sour cream
$^1/_3$ cup caster sugar
2 tsp vanilla extract

1. Preheat the oven to 200°C and grease a 25cm round springform tin (preferably non-stick). Line the base pan with baking paper if you're worried about the crust sticking.
2. For the crust, combine the biscuits, sugar and butter in a food processor. Process until finely ground. An alternative if you do not have a food processor is to place the biscuits into a bag and bang it against a hard surface until it resembles fine breadcrumbs. Empty into a bowl, add the butter and sugar and mix.

3. Press the mixture over the base of the prepared tin and bake for 5 minutes. Reduce the temperature to 175°C and bake for another 5 minutes, then remove, leaving the oven on.

4. To make the filling, use an electric mixer to beat the cream cheese until fluffy, then add the sugar and mix for 2 minutes. Add the flour, lemon zest and salt, and beat for a further 1 minute.

5. Scrape the edges of the bowl to make sure you've mixed all of the ingredients thoroughly, then add the vanilla. Add the eggs one at a time, making sure to mix through after each addition.

6. With the mixer running, slowly pour in the cream. Mix well.

7. Pour the filling into the pan over the crust and bake for 40 minutes. Turn off the oven and allow the cheesecake to sit in the oven for 15 minutes, cooling off slowly.

8. For the topping, whisk the ingredients together. Remove the cheesecake from the oven and turn back on to 175°C. Pour the topping onto the cheesecake, and return to the oven for 6 minutes. Cool to room temperature, then refrigerate overnight (or at least 5 hours).

Easy pastry crust

This recipe makes enough pastry for a double crust pie – top and base. If you want to use it for just base pastry, like in an open tart, halve the quantities. This pastry is great for sweet pies such as apple or chocolate.

PREPARATION TIME: 15 MINUTES + 1 HOUR CHILLING
COOKING TIME: 25 MINUTES
MAKES: 23CM DOUBLE CRUST PIE PASTRY

480g softened butter, chopped
340g cream cheese, at room temperature, chopped
4 cups plain flour, sifted
1 tbsp sugar (for a savoury pie add only $^1/_4$ tsp instead)

1. Combine the butter, cream cheese, flour and sugar in a bowl. Using your hands, rub the ingredients together until combined, and gather the dough into a ball. Wrap in cling wrap and refrigerate for 1 hour.
2. Preheat the oven to 170°C and grease a 23cm pie dish.
3. Roll out half the pastry between 2 sheets of baking paper. Line the dish with the pastry. To blind bake, cover the pastry with a sheet of baking paper and fill with pie weights or uncooked rice.
4. Bake for 15 minutes, then remove the paper and weights and cook a further 8–10 minutes, until the pastry is dry and lightly golden. Remove from the oven and set aside to cool.
5. Fill as directed in your recipe. To make a double crust pie, roll out the remaining pastry and use to cover the filling. Press the edges to seal, and cook as directed.

NOTE: Blind baking ensures that the pastry won't become soggy on the bottom, and is advised even when making a double crust pie. Use a little lightly beaten egg to attach the uncooked top pastry to the cooked base pastry for best results.

Bloody Mary

I love this cocktail and I've included it because it also works really well as a Virgin Mary.

MAKES 1 TALL GLASS

1^1/$_2$ cup tomato juice
1 tsp Tabasco
1 teaspoon Worcestershire sauce
^{1}/$_2$ tsp salt
sprinkle of freshly ground black pepper
splash of vodka (for a Virgin Mary, leave out the vodka)
2 celery sticks
1 lemon slice

Combine juice, Tabasco, Worcestershire sauce, salt, pepper and vodka. Shake well and serve over ice, garnished with celery and lemon.

Green smoothie

This drink is a necessity in my busy life and is also great post-workout. I absolutely love the taste. The blended frozen banana tastes as good as ice-cream.

PREPARATION TIME: 5 MINUTES
SERVES: 1

$1^3/_4$ cups almond milk
1 cup baby spinach leaves (a large handful)
2 tsp flaxseed oil
1 large ripe frozen banana
1 tbsp whey protein (optional)
1 tsp Maca powder (optional)

Combine all the ingredients in a blender and blend for 1 minute or until well combined. Enjoy immediately.

NOTE: I peel and place a few ripe bananas into a container, then I place them into the freezer. That way I can make a few smoothies throughout the week.

Popcorn

Who doesn't love popcorn? I think it's the aroma that gets you. Once I catch a whiff of it at the movies, I have to buy it. I recently scored a popcorn machine from my partner, and this is his mother's recipe. It was a little strange at first, but now I only make my popcorn this way.

PREPARATION TIME: 5 MINUTES
COOKING TIME: 5 MINUTES
SERVES: 2

1/2 cup popping corn
1/3 cup butter (salted or unsalted)
1 heaped tbsp savoury yeast or savoury yeast flakes
3 tsp soy sauce

1. Following popcorn machine instructions, make a large bowl of popcorn. Melt the butter, and coat the popcorn evenly.
2. Sprinkle the yeast and soy sauce over the popcorn. Serve immediately.

NOTE: Look for savoury yeast flakes at the health food shop.

Lindt vanilla cupcakes

This is the traditional vanilla cupcake with a twist! Adding the Lindt chocolate inside is a little unexpected treat.

PREPARATION TIME: 30 MINUTES + 30 MINUTES CHILLING
COOKING TIME: 15–20 MINUTES
MAKES: 20 CUPCAKES

1 cup caster sugar
1 vanilla bean, split, seeds scraped
1^1/$_2$ cups plain flour
1^1/$_2$ tsp baking powder
^{1}/$_2$ tsp bicarb soda
60g salted butter, room temperature, chopped
2 large eggs, room temperature
^{1}/$_3$ cup sour cream
60ml canola or vegetable oil
1 tbsp vanilla extract
160ml milk
20 white chocolate Lindt balls

Vanilla buttercream icing:

125g butter, room temperature, chopped
100g cream cheese, room temperature, chopped
3 tsp vanilla extract
3^3/$_4$ cups icing sugar
3 tbsp milk
8 white chocolate Lindt balls

1. Preheat the oven to 175°C and line 20 cupcake tins with paper cases.
2. In a small bowl, combine the sugar and seeds from the vanilla bean. Using your hands, make sure the vanilla seeds are well combined with the sugar.
3. Combine the flour, baking powder and bicarb soda in a mixing bowl. Add the vanilla bean sugar and mix until well combined. Add the butter and, using an electric mixer, beat on medium-low speed for three minutes, until the mixture resembles fine crumbs.
4. In a small mixing bowl, whisk together the eggs, sour cream, oil and vanilla extract until smooth. Add to the flour mixture and beat on medium speed until just combined. Slowly add the milk and mix on low speed until just combined.
5. Fill the cupcake cases to just over half full, then add a Lindt chocolate ball to each. Cover with more batter until they are just over three quarters full. Bake for 15–20 minutes, until the cupcakes have risen, and their tops are golden. Transfer to a wire rack to cool.

FOR THE ICING:

6. Combine the butter, cream cheese, vanilla, icing sugar and 2 tablespoons of the milk in a bowl. Gently melt the Lindt chocolate balls together with the remaining milk in the microwave or in a bowl over a pan of simmering water until smooth.

7. Using an electric mixer, whip the ingredients in the bowl together for about 3 minutes, slowly adding the melted mixture. Refrigerate for 30 minutes, then pipe onto the cooled cupcakes.

Gingerbread

Every year I make a gingerbread house with gingerbread men. It's a lot of fun to make but very time-consuming.

Two years ago, when I was visiting Australia, I decided to make a gingerbread apartment as I no longer was living in Australia but an apartment in New York. I decided to base it on my actual building. It took days of construction and it was huge.

On Christmas day, when I finally finished, I suddenly realised I had no way of transporting it. I had to carry it the entire way in the car to my cousin's house for Christmas lunch.

As we crossed every speed bump or corner I imagined the whole cake tumbling down. We survived the journey. It wasn't until we arrived that the cake did indeed decide to fall.

I walked into my cousin's Christmas lunch holding the ruins of an apartment. It might not have looked so good, but it still tasted great.

In America they tend to use molasses to make their gingerbread. I tried this once and couldn't believe the stark difference in flavour to something like golden syrup, which is what I've always used.

Golden syrup, in my opinion, makes a crowd-pleasing gingerbread, while molasses is more of a bitter-tasting recipe. I have to buy litres of golden syrup online, as they don't sell it in America, but it's easily available in most Australian supermarkets.

This recipe is for gingerbread cookies. If you are making a gingerbread house (or a similar architectural construction), you'll need four times the amount of this gingerbread.

Gingerbread cookies

PREPARATION TIME: 50 MINUTES
COOKING TIME: 10-15 MINUTES
MAKES: 15-20

125g salted butter, at room temperature, chopped
$^3/_4$ cup firmly packed brown sugar
$^3/_4$ cup golden syrup
1 egg yolk (keep the white for the icing)
$2^1/_2$ cups plain flour
$1^1/_2$ tbsp ground ginger
1 tbsp ground cinnamon
1 tsp bicarb soda

For the icing:

1 egg white
1 cup sifted icing sugar
lollies of your choice, to decorate, optional

1. Preheat the oven to 175°C and line 2 large baking trays with baking paper.
2. Using an electric mixer, beat the butter and sugar in a large bowl until it becomes pale and creamy.
3. Add the golden syrup and egg yolk and continue to mix until combined.
4. Sift the flour, ginger, cinnamon and bicarb soda into the bowl. Mix with a wooden spoon until combined, then turn the dough onto a lightly floured surface and knead briefly until smooth. Shape the dough into a ball and wrap in cling wrap. Refrigerate for 30 minutes.
5. Roll the dough out on a floured surface until it is 2cm thick. For a crispier cookie roll the dough out thinner. Cut out the cookies using a gingerbread man cookie cutter (or other shapes). If you are building a house you can find templates online or draw your own.
6. Place onto the trays and bake for 10–15 minutes, until brown. Transfer to a wire rack to cool.

FOR THE ICING:

7. Using an electric mixer, beat the egg white until soft peaks form. Gradually add the icing sugar, beating constantly. Add a little water if it is too stiff, or a little icing sugar if too runny.
8. Place the icing in a piping bag with a fine nozzle. Use to decorate the cookies, and leave to set. You can also use this icing as the 'glue' for the building of the gingerbread house.

Notes

Toblerone cheesecake

I kind of made this by accident once. I was testing chilled cheesecakes, as baked cheesecakes often crack because of unreliable ovens. This has a great chocolate mousse taste that is lighter than a traditional cheesecake.

PREPARATION TIME: 30 MINUTES + 5 HOURS CHILLING
COOKING TIME: 10 MINUTES
SERVES: 8

Base:
375g Scotch Finger biscuits
100g Toblerone, broken up
125g butter, melted

Filling:
750g cream cheese, at room temperature, chopped
395g can sweetened condensed milk
1 tsp vanilla extract
2 tbsp cocoa powder

Topping (optional):
$3/4$ cup thickened cream
1 tbsp icing sugar

extra Toberlone for decoration (optional)

1. Preheat the oven to 180°C and lightly grease a 23cm springform tin.
2. To make the base, place the biscuits into a food processor and process until crumbs form. Add the Toblerone and butter and process until combined. Press the mixture over the base of the prepared tin.
3. Bake for 10 minutes then cool before filling (I usually pop it in the freezer).
4. For the filling, use an electric mixer at medium speed to beat the cream cheese until smooth. Slowly add the condensed milk, vanilla extract and cocoa, beating until combined. Pour the filling over the base and smooth the surface.
5. Cover and refrigerate for at least 5 hours. When ready to serve carefully remove the sides of the tin – I usually leave the base of the springform on as it can be tricky to remove.
6. Using electric beaters beat the cream and icing sugar together. Once whipped add on top carefully, and decorate with Toblerone pieces.

Red velvet layer cake

This cake is very popular in New York. I'd seen it before in movies but had never tried it, until one day on a photo shoot, when we were served red velvet cake for dessert.

It's a traditional Southern dish, but was also made popular by the Waldorf Astoria. They say the original reason the cake was red was because the buttermilk and vinegar brought out the anthocyanin in cocoa.

Some people also use beetroot to get the red colour. I use beetroot in other chocolate cake recipes, but for this recipe I just use red food colouring to give it a bold red colour.

PREPARATION TIME: 40 MINUTES
COOKING TIME: 25 MINUTES
SERVES: 10+

4^1/$_2$ cups plain flour
6 tbsp Dutch (dark) cocoa powder
2^1/$_2$ tsp baking powder
2 tsp bicarb soda
2^1/$_2$ cups buttermilk
3 tbsp vegetable oil
2 tbsp red food colouring
2 tsp white vinegar
250g salted butter, at room temperature, chopped
3 cups caster sugar
4 eggs
1 tbsp vanilla extract

Icing:
750g cream cheese, room temperature, chopped
185g unsalted butter, room temperature, chopped
4 tsp vanilla extract
6 cups icing sugar, sifted

1. Preheat the oven to 180°C. Grease two 23cm (identical-sized) cake tins and line the bases with baking paper.
2. Sift the flour, cocoa powder, baking powder and bicarb soda into a bowl.
3. Whisk the buttermilk, oil, food colouring and vinegar until blended. It needs to be a very strong red colour, so you may need to add more food colouring as necessary.

4. Using an electric mixer, beat the butter and sugar together in a large bowl until it turns pale, then add the eggs one at a time, beating between each addition. Beat in the vanilla.

5. Reduce the mixer speed to low and beat in the dry ingredients in several batches, alternating with the buttermilk mixture.

6. Pour equal amounts of batter into each tin and bake for 25 minutes. Test with a cake tester before removing, then turn out onto a wire rack to cool.

7. For the icing, beat the cream cheese and butter in a large bowl until smooth, then add the vanilla.

8. Add the icing sugar and continue to beat until smooth.

9. To layer the cake, spread 1 cup of icing over the base of one of the cakes (the flat side), then place the other cake directly on top, right side up. Spread the remaining icing over the top and sides of the cake.

Bread pudding is something I always order if I see it on the menu. The bourbon sauce in this recipe is so delicious and rich it works perfectly with the soft pudding.

Bread pudding with banana and bourbon butter sauce

PREPARATION TIME: 20 MINUTES
COOKING TIME: 40 MINUTES
SERVES: 6–8

Pudding:

melted unsalted butter, to grease
6-7 cups of bread cut into 2cm cubes
4 cups milk
3 eggs, lightly beaten
2 cups sugar
1 tsp vanilla extract
1/4 tsp ground allspice
2 tsp ground cinnamon
3 bananas, chopped

Bourbon butter sauce:

125g salted butter, chopped
1/2 cup sugar
1/4 cup bourbon
1/4 cup thickened cream

1. For the pudding, preheat the oven to 175°C. Grease a 32 x 23 x 5cm baking dish generously with melted butter. Alternatively, for a party, you could use individual ovenproof cups.

2. Combine the bread and milk in a large mixing bowl. Leave to soak until the bread has absorbed all the milk.

3. In a separate bowl, beat the eggs, sugar, vanilla and spices together. Gently stir the egg mixture into the bread mixture, and add the bananas. Transfer to the prepared dish.

4. Bake for 35 minutes or until the edges of the bread are slightly brown on top, and the egg has set at the centre.

5. To make the bourbon sauce, melt the butter in a saucepan, then add the sugar. While stirring, add the bourbon and cream, then keep on the heat until the sauce has thickened slightly. Pour the bourbon sauce on top of the pudding, and serve hot from the oven.

NOTE: The best bread to use is a day-old French or Italian loaf – I use either.

White chocolate panna cotta with berry compote

This is a very decadent panna cotta. I've included a plain recipe as well because I enjoy both variations. This lovely Italian dessert goes down a treat on a spring afternoon.

PREPARATION TIME: 30 MINUTES
COOKING TIME: 10 MINUTES + 6 HOURS SETTING
SERVES: 8

600ml thickened cream
250g good-quality white chocolate, broken up
1 tbsp caster sugar
1 tsp vanilla extract
3 tsp gelatine powder
2 tbsp boiling water
200g plain Greek-style yoghurt

Berry compote:

450g fresh berries
1/3 cup caster sugar
1/4 cup boiling water

1. Combine the cream, chocolate, sugar and vanilla in a saucepan. Stir over very low heat until the chocolate melts and the consistency is smooth. Set aside for 5 minutes.
2. Whisk the gelatine and boiling water in a small bowl with a fork until dissolved. Cool slightly, then stir into the cream mixture. Combine well and cool for 10 minutes.
3. Add the yoghurt and whisk together. Pour the mixture into 8 serving glasses – I used cocktail glasses. Cover and refrigerate for 6 hours or until set.
4. To make the berry compote, combine the berries, sugar and water together in a saucepan and simmer until the liquid reduces and thickens.
5. Place into a bowl, cover and refrigerate until required.
6. Decorate the panna cotta with the compote when ready to serve.

Easy panna cotta

PREPARATION TIME: 20 MINUTES
COOKING TIME: 10 MINUTES + 6 HOURS SETTING
SERVES: 8

1$\frac{1}{2}$ cups thickened cream
1$\frac{1}{2}$ cups milk
$\frac{1}{2}$ teaspoon vanilla extract
$\frac{1}{2}$ cup caster sugar
2$\frac{1}{2}$ tsp gelatine powder
2 tbsp boiling water
fresh berries, to serve

1. Place the cream and milk in a saucepan. Slowly bring to the boil over medium heat, then remove and let cool for 10 minutes.
2. Add the vanilla extract and sugar to the cream mixture and stir over low heat for 5 minutes until the sugar has dissolved. Set aside.
3. Whisk the gelatine and boiling water in a small bowl with a fork, until dissolved. Whisk into the cream mixture, then pour into 8 lightly oiled ramekins. Refrigerate for at least 6 hours, until set.
4. When you are ready to serve the panna cotta, tip it upside down and serve on a plate with fresh berries. You could also set these in glasses for serving, instead of turning out.

Ultimate pie

This interesting pie, which may not look the most photogenic, is derived from the infamous 'crack pie' by Momofuku milk bar in New York. It's so delicious with a combination of sweet and salty flavours, you will be going back for more.

PREPARATION TIME: 40 MINUTES
COOKING TIME: 65 MINUTES
SERVES: 10

Crust:

180g salted butter, at room temperature, chopped
2 tbsp white sugar
5$\frac{1}{2}$ tbsp brown sugar
1 egg
$\frac{3}{4}$ cup rolled oats
$\frac{1}{2}$ cup plain flour
2 tsp ground cinnamon
$\frac{1}{4}$ tsp baking powder
$\frac{1}{4}$ tsp bicarb soda
40 grams butter, chopped

Filling:

$\frac{3}{4}$ cup white sugar
$\frac{1}{2}$ cup brown sugar
1 tbsp skim milk powder
125g salted butter, melted, cooled slightly
4 egg yolks
$\frac{1}{2}$ cup thickened cream
1 tsp vanilla extract
icing sugar, for dusting

1. To make the crust, preheat the oven to 175°C. Lightly grease a 32 x 23cm baking tray and line with baking paper.
2. Combine 120g of the butter with the white sugar and 4 tbsp of the brown sugar. Beat with an electric mixer until the mixture is light and fluffy. Add the egg and beat until the mixture is pale.
3. Add the oats, flour, cinnamon, baking powder and bicarb soda and mix for about 1 minute or until well combined. Transfer to the prepared tray and press out evenly to the edges. Bake for 15 minutes or until lightly golden. Place onto a rack to cool completely. Leave the oven on.

4. Line a 23cm pie dish with baking paper. Crumble the cooled oat mixture into a large bowl. Add the remaining brown sugar and butter. Using your fingertips, rub the sugar and butter with the crumbled oat mixture until it resembles breadcrumbs. Press the mixture evenly onto bottom and up sides of the prepared pie dish.

5. For the filling, combine the sugars and milk powder. Add the melted butter and whisk until blended. Add the yolks, cream and vanilla until well blended. Pour the mixture into the pie crust.

6. Bake for 30 minutes then reduce temperature to 160°C and bake for a further 20 minutes. The mixture should have brown spots and be set around the sides. The centre will still move when shaken (this sets in the fridge). Cool the pie for 2 hours on a rack then refrigerate overnight. Sift icing sugar over the pie and serve cold.

S'mores cupcakes

A S'more is an American treat usually enjoyed around a campfire. It consists of toasted marshmallows and melted chocolate squished between two graham crackers (which are kind of like digestive biscuits). This takes the general idea and turns it into a show-stopping cupcake.

PREPARATION TIME: 40 MINUTES
COOKING TIME: 20 MINUTES
MAKES: 12

Base:

12 Scotch Finger biscuits
125g butter, melted

Filling:

$1^1/_2$ cups plain flour
1 cup caster sugar
2 tbsp Dutch (dark) cocoa powder
$1^1/_2$ tsp baking powder
$^1/_2$ tsp bicarb soda
60g salted butter, at room temperature, chopped
2 eggs, at room temperature
$^1/_3$ cup sour cream
$^1/_4$ cup canola oil
1 tsp vanilla extract
$^2/_3$ cup milk
1 cup small milk or dark chocolate bits, plus extra to decorate (smaller than chocolate chips, if you can find them)

Marshmallow frosting:

2 cups caster sugar
8 large egg whites
$^1/_2$ tsp cream of tartar
2 tsp vanilla extract

1. Preheat the oven to 175°C and line 12 cupcake tins with paper cases.

2. To make the base, place the Scotch Finger biscuits into a food processor and process to fine crumbs. Add the melted butter and process until combined. Spoon the mixture into the base of each paper case, pressing firmly. Set aside.

3. For the filling, sift the flour, sugar, cocoa powder, baking powder and bicarb soda into a medium mixing bowl or the bowl of a stand mixer. Add the butter and mix on medium-low speed for three minutes or until it resembles fine crumbs.

4. In a small mixing bowl, whisk together the eggs, sour cream, oil and vanilla until smooth. Add to the flour mixture and beat on medium speed until just combined. Slowly add the milk, mixing on low speed until just combined. Mix in the chocolate bits.

5. Spoon the mixture into the paper cases over the biscuit base, to just over half to three-quarters full.

6. Bake for 15–18 minutes or until risen, springy to a gentle touch and a rich brown colour. Lift out and set aside to cool.

7. To make the frosting, place all the ingredients into a saucepan and whisk over medium-low heat until the sugar has dissolved. Remove from the heat. Use a hand-held electric mixer in the saucepan (or transfer to the bowl of a stand mixer) to whisk on low speed for about 1 minute, then gradually increase the mxer speed until high. Keep mixing for 5–7 minutes or until stiff peaks start forming. Pipe the frosting onto the cupcakes and add some small chocolate bits.

NOTE: A trick to see if the frosting is ready is to turn the bowl or saucepan upside down – if the mixture is set it won't move. Just don't do it above your head!

Chocolate semifreddo

This lovely recipe popped up on my Tumblr feed two years ago. I get a lot of my inspiration from other cooking blogs, although at times it can be depressing – especially if I'm stuck in a hotel with no kitchen access.

PREPARATION TIME: 30 MINUTES
COOKING TIME: 5 MINUTES + 6 HOURS FREEZING
MAKES: 4

Crust:

250g chocolate wafer biscuits (dark chocolate if possible)
3/4 cup sugar
140g salted butter, melted

Filling:

2 tbsp plus 1/4 cup sugar
350g dark chocolate, chopped
1 tbsp Dutch (dark) cocoa powder
4 egg yolks
1 cup thickened cream
1 cup mascarpone
whipped cream and shaved chocolate, to serve (optional)

1. Preheat the oven to 175°C and lightly grease 4 mini springform tins (12cm diameter x 4cm deep).
2. To make the crust, place the wafers and sugar into a food processor and process to form crumbs. Add the butter and process until combined. Press about 3 tablespoons of mixture into the base of each springform tin. Place tins on a baking tray and bake for 5 minutes. Set aside to cool.
3. For the filling, combine the 2 tbsp sugar with 1/4 cup water in a small saucepan. Stir over medium heat without boiling until the sugar dissolves. Take off the heat and add the chocolate and cocoa powder. Stir until completely smooth. Transfer to a large bowl to cool.
4. Using an electric mixer, beat the egg yolks and remaining sugar for about 5 minutes or until thick, pale and increased in volume. Gently fold into the cooled chocolate mixture.
5. Beat the cream and mascarpone in a separate bowl on high speed until soft peaks form. Gently fold the cream into the chocolate mixture. Pour the mixture evenly into the 4 tins. Cover with cling wrap and freeze for 6 hours or until firm.
6. Remove from freezer 15 minutes prior to serving, to soften slightly. Run a knife around the edge of the semifreddo and carefully remove sides from tins. Slide onto plates and serve with whipped cream and shaved chocolate.

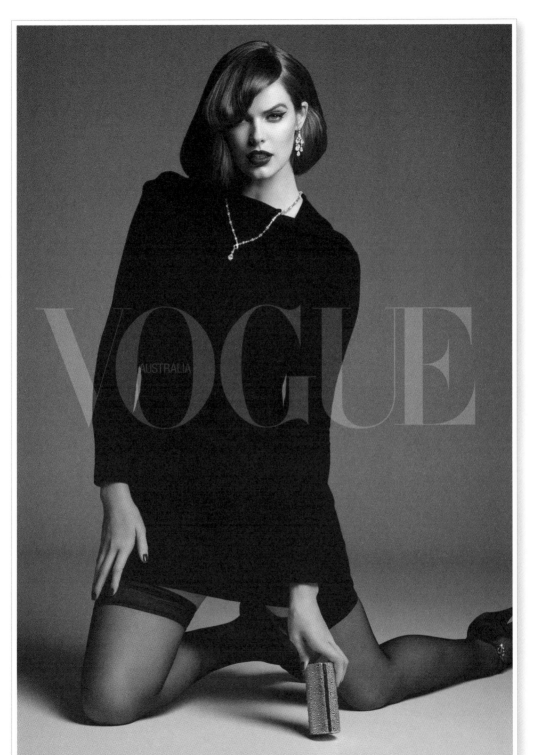

Index

An Ebury Press book
Published by Random House Australia Pty Ltd
Level 3, 100 Pacific Highway, North Sydney NSW 2060
www.randomhouse.com.au

First published by Ebury Press in 2014

Addresses for companies within the Random House Group can be found at www.randomhouse.com.au/offices

Cataloguing-in-Publication entry can be found at the National Library of Australia

ISBN: 978 0 85798 047 2

Cover and internal design by Robyn Lawley with Vivien Valk

Cover photography: © Steven Chee/*Cosmopolitan* magazine Australia

Back cover and internal flaps: Robyn Lawley

All internal food photography and styling by Robyn Lawley, all family photos supplied by Robyn Lawley

Model photos: p iv © Claudio Rashchella; p 1 photo of Robyn at the markets © Claudio Raschella; p 82 © Steven Chee/*Cosmopolitan* magazine Australia; p 84 © Steven Chee/ *Cosmopolitan* magazine Australia; p 85 Kane Skennar/*Cosmopolitan* magazine Australia; p 113 © *Elle* magazine France; p 114–115 © Kane Skennar; p 188 © Steven Chee/ *Cosmopolitan* magazine Australia; p189 © Max Doyle/*Vogue* Australia

Food editing by Tracy Rutherford

Printed in China by 1010 Printing International Co. Ltd.